Dispelling the Myth of "Facts vs. Faith"

Is *Not* a
Four-letter
Word

JAY SEEGERT

STARTING POINT
PUBLISHERS

I spent a lot of time while writing this book thinking about why my faith is so strong and why I am in fulltime ministry today. Ultimately, it is because of God's grace and sovereignty, but He uses people and events in carrying out His will along the way.

The two biggest influences in my life, by far, were my parents, Don and Lois Seegert. I was actually saved during a Backyard Bible Club led by my mom when I was 5 years old!

I learned a lot from listening to them, but even more from watching them! I hope I can provide even half that influence within my own family and I am so comforted knowing I will see my mom and dad again in heaven. (I'm kind of counting on that not actually happening today, but you never know and I'm ready either way!)

Contents

1

Dishwashers and Rest Stops

Returning from a day of routine errands, my wife, Amy, pulled into the garage, gathered her belongings, and walked into the house. She opened the door only to find me standing in the kitchen staring at her with a half-panicked look on my face. "It's alright," I exclaimed, "I've got it under control!" "You've got *what* under control?" Amy asked as she walked nervously toward me. To her surprise, an enormous mound of soap suds drifted in front of the dishwasher with plenty more foaming from all sides. Then she asked, "What were you thinking?" which is usually a rhetorical question in our relationship. I just figured that since (a) we were out of dishwashing soap, and (b) we had plenty of hand soap, it made sense to make a simple substitution – I mean, what could go wrong? Needless to say, my wife is occasionally a bit concerned about me handling things on my own.

On another occasion, I had a speaking engagement about an hour from home, but my wife could not attend because of prior commitments. At the time, our kids were young (about

six and seven), and I needed to take them with me. While en route, I found it necessary to use a rest stop, but since I was already running a bit late, I didn't feel I had enough time to get the kids out of their car seats and bring them with me. I thought to myself, "I'm a guy. I can just leave them in the locked car while I run in, because I can be in and out in about 60 seconds. What could possibly happen?" Other cars were around, and I really felt it would be safe. Saying a quick prayer, I ran in and came back out in record time, only to find they were gone! Not just my kids but my car, too! My heart sank. My mind was racing a million miles an hour! Then, I noticed all the other cars were gone as well, and I started to panic. Suddenly, it hit me. In my haste, I had run out the backside of the rest area! It looked identical to the front, except the parking area was deserted. Frantically, I turned around and ran out the front. My car was parked exactly where I left it, but the kids had done something to set off the car alarm, and they were both crying at the top of their lungs.

No, I'm not the world's worst dad. I share these stories to say that even though I can mess-up from time-to-time, my wife still has faith in me and feels that I am a very good father. Why would she have faith in me even though I make mistakes? There are numerous reasons, but the point in this example is to contrast the kind of faith one person has in another (like the faith my wife has in me) against the kind of faith Christians have in God. There certainly are some similarities, but there are also enormous differences, as you will see throughout the remainder of this book.

My Personal Background

Undoubtedly, your concept of faith will be shaped by your surroundings and circumstances, as were mine.

I grew up in a Christian home where faith was a huge part of our lives. It wasn't just something that shaped our Sundays, but it influenced my family throughout the week. I was very fortunate to have parents who not only were Christians but who also demonstrated Christianity in every aspect of their lives. Faith was something I was taught <u>and</u> something I *caught*. I realize not everyone has that kind of an upbringing. In fact, most don't. Often, even many living in Christian homes are taught only a minimal amount about the Bible and rarely see it consistently lived out in the lives of those around them.

While I believe that true faith is a gift from God, I also recognize God gives some the specific "gift of faith" (1 Corinthians 12:8-10). I believe that I might have that gift primarily because it is easy for me to trust God and not worry about the future or specific situations. On the other hand, sometimes I wonder if it's more apathy and complacency. There can be a fine line between the two. I'd like to say it's actually faith, so let's go with that!

Main Goals of this Book

Every great writer has *three* main goals they wish to achieve. With that in mind, here are my *four* goals for this book:

1. To dispel the myth of "Facts vs. Faith."
2. To train Christians to powerfully defend their faith without needing degrees in physics, astronomy, history, Greek or Hebrew, etc., and without having to memorize a lot of facts.
3. To share some practical advice on how to put what you will learn here into practice in your everyday life.
4. To position you so others never successfully pressure you into believing that sharing your faith is like using a four-letter word!

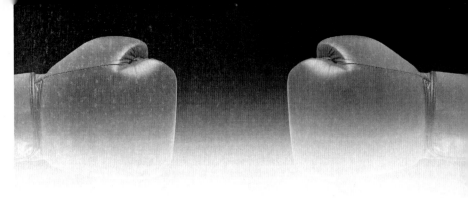

2

The "Facts vs Faith" Dilemma

We've all been there. You're having a conversation, in which deep down inside, you know your case is weak, but you don't want to admit it or show any vulnerability. When you lack a good defense, you can always resort to becoming more emotional, right? Actually, that's not usually an effective response, and even if it seems to work at the time, it's not an adequate substitute for a compelling argument. Consider the following conversation.

Skeptic: "Evolution is a fact and the Bible is just mythology!"

Christian: "I don't believe that. I think creation is true and the Bible is the inspired Word of God."

Skeptic: "Prove it! Give me one fact that proves creation is true or that the Bible is actually from God."

Christian: "Well, I don't know that I can prove
                it, but that's what I believe."

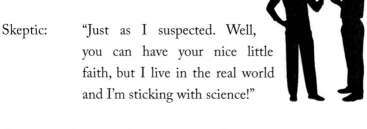

Skeptic: "Just as I suspected. Well,
                you can have your nice little
                faith, but I live in the real world
                and I'm sticking with science!"

Can you relate to this scenario? Perhaps you've experienced
something like this yourself or you know someone who has.

When this is all the further the conversation goes, the skeptic feels
justified in holding to their skepticism and doesn't think very highly
of the Christian's level of intelligence or competence. It also leaves
the Christian frustrated and embarrassed, not wanting to ever get
into that situation again, avoiding it at all costs. In some cases, it
causes the Christian to lose confidence in the Bible, even to the
extent of walking away from their faith in God.

Here's an important question. Do you want to find answers? Not
everyone does. Why can't a thief find a police officer? Oh yeah, he's
not looking for one! So too, when people say, "I would have done
this or that, but I just didn't have the time," what they really mean
is, "I didn't do this or that because it wasn't important enough to
me." Here's the point. Like the thief who can't find a police officer,
Christians can't find answers because they are not looking for them.
Culture has taught them that amid scientific academia, their faith is
as bad as a four-letter word; that faith is nothing more than a rule
book they shouldn't have to follow. The result?

Today, many Christian youth walk away from their faith before they finish college. In fact, they are abandoning their faith at younger and younger ages. Many of them walk away because, ultimately, they don't *want* answers to the challenges that have come their way. When we naïvely assume they left the faith because they did not have answers for challenging questions, we often miss the real reason. Fairly regularly, when Christian youth are drawn away by the lures of the world, the arguments against Christianity sound very powerful and persuasive, and those arguments also come in very handy when trying to justify walking away. In these cases, Christian young people are not looking for answers and often respond adversely when anyone attempts to offer answers for the critics' arguments. This leads young believers to view faith as weak in comparison to the defense for a more humanistic worldview.

My Own Story

Even though I attended public school through high school, I still lived within a comfortable Christian bubble. I went to church three times a week, was always in some type of youth group, and had many Christian friends. I even attended a Christian college (John Brown University in Arkansas) to get a degree in Engineering Technology. All of this meant that I was very seldom challenged regarding my beliefs. That changed, however, when I transferred to a state university in Wisconsin to get a degree in physics. My professors told me I was wrong about everything I believed! That made me feel extremely uncomfortable! I realized for the first time in my entire life that even though I knew what I believed by faith, I did not know why. I was not able to defend my Christian worldview. I assumed my professors had evidence for their beliefs, but I felt I had virtually none for my own views. As an aside, I discovered later my professors did not truly have evidence for what they believed. My professors accepted their beliefs by faith, too, even though they would never admit to that or see it that way themselves.

When I was greatly challenged in my faith, what happened to me? It is at this point that a high percentage of Christian youth today end up walking away. Did I walk away? No! Quite the opposite! (I don't say that arrogantly or to give myself any credit. I simply wish to emphatically state that my reaction sits in stark contrast to today's youth leaving the faith.) Why didn't I walk away?

I have been researching and lecturing on the Christian worldview for over 35 years now. That includes addressing the tragic trend of Christian youth walking away from the faith. However, it wasn't until just a few years ago that I asked myself the question, "Why didn't I walk away at that point in my life?" It took me about half of a second to figure out the answer. It was my relationship with my parents! I don't think it had anything to do with my level of education or even my level of Christian maturity, which I'm sure was nowhere close to where it was supposed to be. I respected my parents so much that I didn't think for one second they were wrong about what they told me or were lying about anything. I also respected my pastor and didn't feel that he was wrong either. Being a fairly logical thinker, I reasoned the following: "If I am not wrong about my views, that means I am right. If I am right, that means there must be evidence. If there is evidence, I'm going to find it!" I was very passionate and intentional about this pursuit. God connected me to someone at my church who was able to answer my questions. The rest is history, including leading to the formation of an international apologetics ministry! As a cool bonus, I still get together with that man for breakfast regularly, now 35 years later!

So, why did I have faith that evidence existed? I believe it was because of the sovereignty of God and a result of making an effort to find evidence that He exists, trusting that He would reward me for diligently seeking Him (Hebrews 11:6).

Fact vs Faith

We are living in a society that constantly pits "facts versus faith." Supposedly, skeptics are all about facts and proving things, while Christians simply have faith, which we're told is nothing more than wishful thinking — rainbows and puppy dogs. At least that's how the skeptics see it. Even some Christians feel this way. They think to themselves, "Well, Christianity is a faith and you just have to believe  it." This attitude yields a weakened view of Christianity and fosters a considerable hesitation regarding sharing their faith with others.

We see examples of the alleged battle of "facts vs faith" in the media and all around us. One example came from a talk show in which the secular host and guests were discussing global warming.[1]

The secular guests shared that there was a "statistical correlation between deniers of global warming and religious believers." Their point was the more religious you are, the more likely you were to deny global warming. They concluded, "Religion clouds the mind of those who, if they were only sufficiently educated, would arrive at the conclusion supported by the overwhelming preponderance of scientific evidence and reject the blind adherence to revealed or ecclesiastical authority that characterizes religious belief."

The guests went on to state that "intellectual responsibility" for most important aspects of life "has passed in the modern era from the Bible to academic departments… We still cite chapter and verse — we still operate on trust — but the scripture has changed (at least in this country) and is now identified with the most up-to-date research conducted by credentialed and secular investigators."

Their point is they believe society needs to get away from the overly restrictive and utterly errant views purported in a book as antiquated as the Bible. This is not a new approach or attitude. It harkens back to before Darwin's time, showing up clearly in a statement by Charles Lyell, who wrote a three-volume treatise entitled, *Principles of Geology*. His stated goal in writing these books was to "free the science from Moses!" I elaborate on this further in our video series, "The Genesis Flood." In a nutshell, Lyell wanted to move away from what the Bible says about creation and the flood. He was piggy-backing on the works of his predecessor, James Hutton, who is considered the Father of Modern Geology. Hutton stated, "The past history of our globe must be explained by what can be seen to be happening now. No powers are to be employed that are not natural to the globe, no action to be admitted except those of which we know the principle."

The supernatural *need not apply*. Hutton and Lyell served to usher in a new era in which the Bible was to take a *back seat* (way, way back seat) to what they were calling science. God was demoted and virtually not needed anymore. The new god-less, higher-science culture now allowed God to *pop His head in* once-in-a-while, albeit to a limited extent, but only with pre-approval from the scientific magisterium.

Even in the Church

This errant view of Christianity has even crept into the church. I saw a sign outside of one church that stated, "Reason is the greatest enemy that faith has!" I think that is a terrible message to be portraying to people driving by! What does Scripture say? "Come now, and let us reason together," Says the Lord" (Isaiah 1:18). God wants us to use our minds. Jesus said we are to "love the Lord your God with all your heart, with all your soul, with all your mind, and with all your strength" (Mark 12:30).

I saw another sign that stated, "If your faith is big enough, facts don't count!" So, what message is this sign portraying? "If your faith is strong enough you don't have to worry about any of those pesky facts or science." Again, what a terrible message to be proclaiming to the public!

If we retain a weakened view of Christianity, we will feel inferior to skeptics who *supposedly* know what they believe and also have a solid, rational defense to back it up. The skeptic is not superior in knowing and defending what he believes. Most are vague and shaky regarding what they believe and miles away from offering a lucid defense.

At a very minimum, Christians should be prepared to explain succinctly and clearly what they believe. It's difficult to defend something that you can't define. Too often, a general lack of basic Bible literacy causes these deficiencies. Developing a defense takes time and effort. The fact that you are reading this book shows you desire to be better positioned to define and defend your faith . . . and that's a great start!

The remainder of this book should go a long way in giving you a better foundation for your faith, so let's keep plugging away!

3

Faith: What It Is and What It Ain't

I walked into the crowded room, took my place up front, and quickly observed that what I had been told was correct. I was invited by a Christian organization to speak to a group of public high school students regarding the Christian faith and was informed that many in attendance were outspoken skeptics. Furthermore, I was told it would not be difficult to distinguish the skeptics from the others. I generally don't "judge a book by its cover," but it wasn't hard spotting them for many reasons. They had physically distanced themselves from everyone else. They also had demeanors distinctly characteristic of someone who is suspicious and unconvinced.

Having been told this group may be particularly challenging, I spontaneously changed my normal routine and opened my presentation with a question. "Is there anyone here who doesn't have faith in anything... nothing at all?" One student immediately and proudly raised her hand. I thanked her for being so open and inquired if I could ask a few follow-up questions to which she agreed.

The following conversation ensued:

Myself: "Tell me, how did you get to school today? Did you
               ride in a car?"

Student: "Yes."

Myself: "Before you got in the car, did you conduct every
               imaginable test on that vehicle to prove beyond the
               shadow of a doubt that it would not explode on the
               way to school, killing you in the process?"

Student: "No, I didn't."

Myself: "So, you had faith the car would not explode."

Student: "Yes, I guess so."

Myself: "Before you entered this building, did you conduct
               an exhaustive structural analysis proving it would not
               collapse while you were here?"

Student: "Of course not."

Myself: "So, you had faith that the building was up to code."

Student: "Sure."

Myself: "Before you entered this room, did you a thorough
               scientific analysis of its atmosphere to guarantee
               there was an appropriate ratio of nitrogen and

oxygen enabling you to breathe properly during the meeting?"

Student: "No."

Myself: "So, you had faith that it was suitable."

Student: "I suppose."

Myself: "In reality, you have faith in quite a few things. And the faith you are exercising is actually a very reasonable faith based on knowledge and prior experience, wouldn't you say?"

Student: "Yes, I think so."

Myself: "And that is exactly my point. Christianity also involves faith (as do all other beliefs systems). However, in the case of Christianity, it is not a blind faith but rather a very reasonable faith based on numerous lines of evidence from history, archaeology, science, prophecy, and more."

At the risk of sounding annoying or condescending, I was simply trying to get her to see that she exercises faith on a regular basis. We all do. I also wanted to emphasis that in most cases our faith is at least somewhat reasonable because of experiences we've had or because strong evidence exists in favor of our belief. During the remainder of my talk I shared examples of powerful evidence for the accuracy and reliability of the Christian faith.

This personal story helps illustrate the fact that there are misconceptions regarding what biblical faith really is (i.e., it's not a blind faith). However, if you ask four different people to define faith in general, you'll probably get five different answers!

Just for Fun

Before we get too serious, I thought it would be fun to take a look at the humorous side of faith by sharing a few admittedly marginally funny stories (from unknown sources).

The Fall

A man named Jack was walking along a steep cliff one day when he accidentally got too close to the edge and fell. On the way down he grabbed a branch which temporarily stopped his fall. He looked down  and to his horror saw that the canyon fell straight down for more than a thousand feet.

He couldn't hang onto the branch forever, and there was no way for him to climb up the steep wall of the cliff. So, Jack began yelling for help, hoping that someone passing by would hear him and lower a rope or something.

"HELP! HELP! Is anyone up there? HELP!"

He yelled for a long time, but no one heard him. He was about to give up when he heard a deep voice. "Jack, Jack. Can you hear me?"

"Yes, yes! I can hear you. I'm down here!"

"I can see you, Jack. Are you all right?"

"Yes, but who are you, and where are you?"

"I am the Lord, Jack. I'm everywhere."

"The Lord? You mean, GOD?"

"That's Me."

"God, please help me! I promise if, you get me out of this situation, I'll stop sinning. I'll be a really good person. I'll serve You for the rest of my life."

"Easy on the promises, Jack. Let me help you out; then we can talk."

"Now, here's what I want you to do. Listen carefully."

"I'll do anything, Lord. Just tell me what to do."

"Okay. Let go of the branch."

"What?"

"I said, let go of the branch. Just trust Me. Let go."

There was a long silence.

Finally, Jack yelled, "HELP! HELP! IS ANYONE ELSE UP THERE?"

It's easy to place our faith in something when we can easily envision it being successful, but when it involves something beyond our comprehension, even something seemingly completely illogical, that's much, much more difficult.

Have Faith My Child

For the umpteenth time Mrs. Youngston came to her pastor to tell him, "I'm so scared! Joe says he's going to kill me if I continue to come to your church."

"Yes, yes, my child," replied the pastor, more than a little tired of hearing this over and over. "I will continue to pray for you, Mrs. Youngston. Have faith — the Lord will watch over you."

"Oh yes, he has kept me safe thus far, only . . ."

"Only what, my child?"

"Well, now he says if I keep coming to your church, he's going to kill YOU!"

"Well, now," said the pastor, "Perhaps it's time to check out that little church on the other side of town."

It's always easier to tell someone else to "just have faith" than to put it into practice ourselves!

Skeptic's View of Faith

Before we jump in and focus on defining what faith actually is, let's take a look at what others think about faith. Skeptics in particular have their own thoughts. Here are just a few examples:

"Faith is NOT a virtue, faith is gullibility, dishonesty, blindness, the absence of reason and not based on facts. Faith should not be respected; it should be detested."
— SOURCE UNKNOWN

"It is time that we admitted that faith is nothing more than the license religious people give one another to keep believing when reasons fail."
— Sam Harris, *Letter to a Christian Nation,* (2006)[2]

"Faith: not wanting to know what is true."
— Friedrich Nietzsche, German philosopher & atheist, *The Joyful Science,* (1882)[3]

"Faith is the great cop-out, the great excuse to evade the need to think and evaluate evidence. Faith is belief in spite of, even because of, the lack of evidence."
— Richard Dawkins, Untitled Lecture, Edinburgh Science Festival (1992)[4]

"Faith is believing in what you know ain't so."
— Mark Twain (*citation details unknown*)[5]

It is more than apparent these skeptics don't think very highly of faith. Paraphrasing Mark Twain, "We know what we believe isn't true, but we're going to believe it anyway. That's what faith is all about!" What a sad and errant view of faith! And as I stated chapter 2, this weakened view has crept into many churches. Remember the signs I mentioned that were out front of two churches? "Reason is the greatest enemy that faith has!" and "If you're faith is big enough, facts don't count!"

Interesting Exercise

Before we go directly into Scripture, I'd like to take you through a very interesting exercise. I want you to read the following paragraph and see what you think about it. Important Note: Don't over-analyze it or stress over it. Simply read it calmly and naturally all the way through and I'll see you on the other side.

> A newspaper is better than a magazine. A seashore is a better place than the street. At first it is better to run than to walk. You may have to try several times. It takes some skill, but it is easy to learn. Even young children can enjoy it. Once successful, complications are minimal. Birds seldom get too close. Rain, however, soaks in very fast. Too many people doing the same thing can also cause problems. One needs lots of room. If there are no complications, it can be very peaceful. A rock will serve as an anchor. If things break loose from it, however, you will not get a second chance.

Most likely, even though you could understand each individual sentence, the paragraph as a whole didn't seem to make much sense.

It seems very random and generally meaningless. Here's the fun part. I want you to re-read the paragraph (reprinted below), but this time as you read, I want you to picture in your mind . . . a kite. Got it? Alright, go ahead and read the paragraph again and see if it all magically comes together.

> A newspaper is better than a magazine. A seashore is a better place than the street. At first it is better to run than to walk. You may have to try several times. It takes some skill, but it is easy to learn. Even young children can enjoy it. Once successful, complications are minimal. Birds seldom get too close. Rain, however, soaks in very fast. Too many people doing the same thing can also cause problems. One needs lots of room. If there are no complications, it can be very peaceful. A rock will serve as an anchor. If things break loose from it, however, you will not get a second chance.

Wasn't that an interesting exercise? (This is where you say, "Yes, Jay, that was great! Thanks so much for sharing it with me!" You can at least pretend to feel that way. I won't know the difference!)

What's the spiritual application? What one sees when considering all that is around them is largely determined by the filter or worldview that they have in mind to begin with. When you first read the sample paragraph, you didn't necessarily have anything in mind as a backdrop or central focal point. Therefore, nothing seemed to make sense. However, once you had something specific in mind, something you related each individual sentence to, it all came together. In reality, no one approaches life (and all that is around them) starting with a "blank slate." We all have a worldview or starting point we use to interpret and to make sense of everything else. If you have the wrong starting point, you will struggle with just about everything in life. For example, imagine you pictured in your mind a German World War II submarine as you read through the exercise paragraph. That would make everything much more confusing, and you'd have to work very hard to make the pieces fit. We will develop this concept further as we discover more about our worldview throughout this book.

My Definition of Faith

Not that this should be very important to anyone else or carry any weight whatsoever, but I simplistically describe biblical faith as, "Believing God is who He says He is, that He did what He said He did, and that He will do what He says He will do." The pervasive underlying assumption to my definition is that the Bible truly is the Word of God, conveying who He is and what He requires of us.

Go Right to the Source

One of the ways God has revealed Himself to us is through nature. Romans 1:20 makes it very clear that there is so much evidence for God's existence, just in nature itself, that we are all without excuse for not knowing Him. That means no one will ever stand before God and say, "Yeah, I would have believed in you, but you didn't give me enough evidence." Humorously, if this was a game show, that's when you would hear the loud "wrong answer" buzzer and the trap door beneath your feet would open, quickly sending you on your way!

As awesome as God's creation is (don't get me started), it is still limited in its ability to communicate. What I mean by that is you can look all day long at morpho butterflies, DNA, or the trillions upon trillions of stars in the universe, and they will never be able to tell you things like, "Who made them?", "Why were they made?" or "What happens to us when we die?" (i.e., "Is there a heaven or hell?"). Answering those types of questions requires something different; something we call "special revelation." Another question that can only be answered by special revelation would be, "What is faith?" God's Word is just that, "special revelation."

If the Bible is the source of our faith, it makes sense to turn to it to define exactly what faith is.

Biblical Definition of Faith

A truly biblical definition of faith is much more important than what I or anyone else might think about faith. I will share some fairly standard passages regarding faith, one of which might take you by surprise. It did me.

The Greek word most often used for faith in the New Testament is **πίστις** (pistis). It appears 244 times in the King James version. Here's how it is translated:

"faith" (239 times)
"assurance" (1 time)
"believe" (1 time)
"belief" (1 time)
"them that believe" (1 time)
"fidelity" (1 time)

Most of the biblical passages concerning faith discuss the act of faith but don't directly define it. As an example:

> For by grace you have been saved through faith, and that not of yourselves; it is the gift of God, not of works, lest anyone should boast (Ephesians 2:8-9).

This verse states that we are saved by the grace of God, and the way in which that occurs is through *faith*. Our salvation is not based on what we've done or our moral standing. It is solely a gift from God; therefore, we cannot brag about it or have any self-pride in having earned it.

I would dare to add another thought here. Since it is clearly indicating that salvation is a gift from God and the way we receive the gift is through faith, I strongly believe *faith itself* is a gift from God. Heres' another great verse emphasizing the same message:

> knowing that a man is not justified by the works of the law but by faith in Jesus Christ, even we have believed in Christ Jesus, that we might be justified by faith in Christ and not by the works of the law; for by the works of the law no flesh shall be justified (Galatians 2:16).

Here's a verse about different types of faith:

> You believe that there is one God. You do well. Even the demons believe—and tremble! (James 2:19).

This verse indirectly makes the important point that there is a significant difference between simply believing something mechanically (i.e., mental ascent) and belief involving agreeing with and being committed to something or someone. Even today, both Christians and Satan believe in God, but there's a HUGE difference between these two beliefs!

Here's a classic verse many Christians have memorized:

> For we walk by faith, not by sight (2 Corinthians 5:7).

This passage tells us we are to walk by faith (whatever that is; not being defined here), as opposed to what we see (which inherently includes using our own reasoning).

The following analogy illustrates how we are not to "lean on our own understanding" (Proverbs 3:5-6) and serves to make a powerful point. Occasionally, when pilots are flying, their vision out the front window is greatly obscured. In extreme situations, they may lose control and not even know whether or not they are right-side up! What they think they see, coupled with whatever their gut instinct is at the time, might tell them to make the wrong adjustments which could lead to disaster! In their training, they are taught to "trust the indicators," even though it might seem counter intuitive.

A pilot's misplaced faith in his feelings instead of his instruments can be similar to the consequences of where we place our trust in our daily lives. At the time, a specific action might seem to make perfect sense, but it might be contrary to trusting what God said. During those times, too often we "think we know better" and make the wrong choice. We'll see an example of this regarding when Abraham tried to "help God out." Abraham's choices ended up yielding disastrous consequences. Ever hear of the Middle East Arab-Israeli conflict? Yep, that goes all the way back to this time when Abraham thought he knew better! That unending warfare is the cataclysmic consequence of one bad choice Abraham made. (See Galatians 4:21–31.)

This next verse gives an important warning:

> that your faith should not be in the wisdom of men but in the power of God (1 Corinthians 2:5).

The concept of trusting God instead of men would have helped Abraham avoid a lot of trouble. But before we are quick to judge Abraham, we need to keep in mind that this truth applies to us as well! We may very well have made the same decision Abraham did given his circumstances.

This verse touches on the consistency of our faith:

> he is a double-minded man, unstable in all his ways (James 1:8).

The emphasis is on the consistency of trusting. If you are prone to doubting and hemming and hawing, you will experience the instability mentioned here in James. It makes living the Christian life much harder than it should be and will also markedly deter you from sharing your faith.

The importance of not doubting is addressed here:

> But he who doubts is condemned if he eats, because he
> does not eat from faith; for whatever is not from faith is sin
> (Romans 14:23).

This passage warns that if you are ever in doubt about something, don't eat that day or you're in BIG trouble! ☺ OK, just a little humor. Actually, that's how many people go off the rails. They take one passage out of context and get hyper-focused on it. That's how many cults start . . . so, don't do that. Maybe you should go get something to eat right now. I'll wait.

The main point of this verse is that whenever you do something, it should be in good faith believing that it's the correct, God-directed choice. Whether it's which job offer to accept, which house to buy, how to appropriately discipline your children, how to respond to a friend, etc., it should be done in good faith. In each case, if you don't have some level of faith/confidence regarding what the right choice is, I would highly recommend spending more time in prayer before making a decision simply because you felt you were pressed to rush the process. You'll be surprised how God will lead you in the right direction if you are truly looking to Him, which might include simply waiting, period! Well, waiting, exclamation point!

An Actual Definition

Arguably, the most lucid passage directly defining faith is found in the book of Hebrews:

> Now faith is the substance of things hoped for, the evidence
> of things not seen (Hebrews 11:1).

Most of you have probably read this passage before, probably multiple times. It is interesting that you can read a verse many times over and still something new can strike you that you never saw before. God reveals more and more as you are committed to studying His Word. (Psalm 119:18 "Open my eyes, that I may see Wondrous things from Your law.")

This happened to me with this verse a few years ago. However, in my case, I think I should have seen this long before. I believe it was due to focusing on merely reading as opposed to truly studying that kept me from seeing this sooner.

According to this verse, it's not about finding evidence for our faith . . . it's saying that our faith *is* the evidence! Really? Read Hebrews 11:1 again.

> Now **faith is** the substance of things hoped for, **the evidence** of things not seen.

This verse is saying that faith is two things: (a) the substance of things hoped for and (b) the evidence of things not seen. Referring to just the second of these two, you can accurately say, "Faith is the evidence of things not seen!" So, in one sense, it's not about finding evidence for our faith; faith *is* the evidence for our faith! It's the evidence indicating that what we believe is actually true! This may sound strange and confusing, so allow me to comment a bit further.

As Christians, the mere fact that we have the kind of faith we do, is evidence that God exists, because only God could give us *that* kind of faith. Again, we're not talking about faith in the simple sense of choosing to believe something even though we can't prove it.

We're talking about having confident assurance!

> These things I have written to you who believe in the name of the Son of God, **that you may know** that you have eternal life, and that you may continue to believe in the name of the Son of God (1 John 5:13).

The Greek words used in this verse convey an assured confidence, not wishful thinking or just being "pretty sure" or "hopeful." John is writing so that we may **know**! The ability to know something for sure is actually a supernatural characteristic. Left to our own devices, the best we could do is gather information, think through it, and then try to be as confident as we can, never really *knowing* with absolute certainty. We'll study another aspect of this in the "Practical Application" section coming up.

Matthew Henry, in his commentary on Hebrews, states, "Faith demonstrates to the eye of the mind the reality of those things that cannot be discerned by the eye of the body."[6]

Secular Version of Hebrews 11:3,6

Let's briefly revisit both of these verses as we see them in Scripture:

> By faith we understand that the worlds were framed by the word of God, so that the things which are seen were not made of things which are visible (v 3).
> But without faith it is impossible to please Him, for he who comes to God must believe that He is, and that He is a rewarder of those who diligently seek Him (v 6).

We've just spent some time looking at the true meaning of these verses. By way of a bit of facetiousness, I want to show you how the world would change these verses if they could:

> "By science we understand that the universe was formed by accident, so that what is seen was not made out of anything super-natural. And without faith it is impossible to please scientists, because anyone who comes to them must believe that they are right and that they reward those who consistently and unquestioningly trust them."
> (*Heathens* 11:3, 6)

Practical Application

I was wrapping-up a 3-hour conversation with a very prestigious atheist when he asked me a basic question that people rarely ask. It's such a basic question you would assume I would be asked all the time. I certainly address this question often in my talks and writing, but rarely does anyone ever ask it point blank. When suddenly being asked this question out-of-the-blue, I did not have a standard answer like I do for many others. I ended up giving him an answer I've never given before. In fact, I didn't even know where I was headed! It was a very strange situation, but I've been there at least one other time, and I learned that God was taking over the steering wheel, so-to-speak. I just had to trust the Holy Spirit to make my words come out sensible. But yes, I am still a sinner whose prideful, natural tendency is to worry about how I might look when it's over. Then I sense God saying, "Relax, Jay. This isn't about you. It's about someone's eternal destiny, and I care about their eternal destiny even more than you."

We (the atheist and I) had spent the majority of the 3-hour conversation discussing why he didn't believe in God, and I purposely had refrained from saying much about my own beliefs. Being the head of an Atheist Association in his home state, he knew a fair amount about Christianity, and we already had done a live radio interview together a few months prior. After the radio show, he asked if we could go out to dinner, but my prior commitment kept me from accepting his invitation. I asked if he would be willing to get together the next time I was in the area and he said, "Yes." About six months later, I was invited back to California and I contacted him about getting together. He enthusiastically agreed to this follow-up meeting. I told him my primary interest was getting to know him better, including finding out more about why he was an atheist.

The day arrived and we met at a local restaurant. I really didn't want it to be an out-and-out debate. I simply wanted both of us to relax and enjoy the time together. About 30 minutes into the discussion he said, "This is great! I wish we could do this every day!" I said, "Yes, isn't it sad that more Christians and atheists can't just have an honest conversation without malice and name-calling?"

What was his question to me at the very end of our lengthy discussion? His facial expression revealed he just realized that after three hours of him telling me why he didn't believe in God, I had never said why I do! So, he point-blank asked, "So, why do *you* believe it God?"

My response was as follows:

> "There are a number of reasons why I believe God exists, but there's one that far exceeds all others. The Bible says that God is a spirit; He's not a physical being. The Scriptures

further state that we are created in God's image. Since God does not have a physical image, what this means is in addition to our physical bodies, we also have a spirit. In Romans 8:16 it tells us, 'The Spirit itself beareth witness with our spirit, that we are the children of God.' This verse reveals that God supernaturally implants from His Spirit to ours the assured knowledge that those who have placed their faith in His Son, Jesus Christ become the children of God. Therefore, I believe I can actually 'know that I know that I know' God exists and that I am a child of His! This isn't something I have reasoned through the use of my own limited abilities. This powerful relationship is something supernaturally instilled in my innermost being. I don't expect you to be impressed by that, seriously. I don't expect you to be impressed with the fact that I think 'I know that I know that I know.' Honestly, that's not for you. That's for me to be confident in my faith and to aid when I am sharing with others or experiencing any of the significant challenges life brings my way. Here's a very important point. If you want to come to God, you'll have to do it on His terms, not yours. If you're waiting to have everything proven to you and then you'll believe, it doesn't work that way. God says in Hebrews 11:6 that those who come to Him must come (a) believing He exists, and (b) believing He will reward those who diligently seek Him. If you want to do it that way, you'll have all the assurance in the world!"

Prior to this, my conversation with this very cordial atheist was non-stop and fluid for the entire three hours! However, at this point he was like a deer staring into headlights! So, why the "deer in the headlights" response? I believe it mostly had to do with the direct sharing of Scripture! Earlier, I shared a few very powerful arguments in response to him explaining his background and beliefs. However, I never got the impression he was significantly fazed by much of it. But when I shared Scripture, that was a different ballgame.

God says His Word will never return void.

> So shall My word be that goes forth from My mouth; It shall not return to Me void, But it shall accomplish what I please, And it shall prosper in the thing for which I sent it (Isaiah 55:11).

It doesn't say that when we share our best, most clever arguments that we will definitely change the skeptic's mind. God will often sovereignly use those arguments as part of someone's change of heart, but it's really the conviction of the Holy Spirit through the sharing of God's Word that does the real, spiritual transformation.

I am still praying for this man. He was very kind, very intelligent, and a lot of fun to talk to. I honestly think he'll make a great Christian some day!

Object vs. Strength

Another important aspect of faith is that it is not the *strength of our faith* that counts so much as it is the *strength of the object* of our faith. We can illustrate this using the following question. Which scenario will result in a more successful outcome?

a) Having incredibly strong faith in the chair on the left.
b) Having even a relatively small amount of faith in the chair on the right?

Assuming you will actually act upon your faith at some point (independent of its strength), the answer is obvious. You can have all the faith in the world the rickety chair will hold you up, but the strength of your faith does not influence the chair's actual ability to support you in the least. On the other hand, as you sit on the granite chair, even though your faith may be small, the chair is fully capable of holding you and is not diminished in any sense because of your tentativeness.

To further illustrate this point, I'll share a somewhat humorous story when my wife was student teaching at a local high school. They had planned a field trip to the Chicago Museum of Science and Industry which was about two hours from where we live in Wisconsin. The school needed some more chaperones, so a friend of mine and I both volunteered. It just happened to be on the day of a very important football game for the Wisconsin Badgers. If they won, they were headed to the Rose Bowl! My friend decided to record the game since we would not be able to watch it live. Many of the students on the bus were wearing headphones, listening to the game on the way to the museum. We informed them of our plans to watch it later and pleaded with them not to tell us what was happening at any point. Throughout the drive down and during the museum tour, various students would tease us and share a few comments about the game, but it was all in good fun, because nothing they said gave any indication of how things were really going.

The tour ended and we loaded the bus to head back home. The game had ended and the students were still teasing us, but not letting on at all as to the outcome. A teacher sitting up front with us noticed the banter of the students and inquired as to what it was all about. I explained the whole situation, and not wanting her to be upset with them, I made it clear that they never did share anything that would ruin our plans to watch the recorded game that evening. She replied by saying, "Yeah, I wasn't following the game myself. All I know is that the Badgers won." I could not believe it! We made it through the entire six-hour field trip with sugar-filled students teasing the whole time, only to have it ruined by one of the teachers! This was a case of having put our faith in the wrong thing. We had trusted the faculty, but not the students, when it apparently should have been the other way around. Overall, somewhat of an insignificant story, but it illustrates the point of making sure your faith is in the right place! And yes, I'm still miffed about my misplaced trust, 20 years later!

In the context of our overall subject, it is the object of our faith (Jesus) that makes all the difference, as opposed to concentrating on the *amount* or *strength* of our faith.

There is a biblical example of someone struggling to believe. It was someone whose request was answered, not because of the strength of his faith (which was lacking), but because of the object of his faith (Jesus). In the book of Mark, we read the story of a man whose son had been possessed by an evil spirit:

> So He asked his father, "How long has this been happening to him?" And he said, "From childhood. And often he has thrown him both into the fire and into the water to

destroy him. But if You can do anything, have compassion on us and help us." Jesus said to him, "If you can believe, all things are possible to him who believes." Immediately the father of the child cried out and said with tears, "Lord, I believe; help my unbelief!" (Mark 9:21-29).

Jesus was pointing out the fact that the father wasn't really sure He could actually heal his son. The man replied that he did believe (at least somewhat), but really needed help increasing his faith. I see this as a very sincere admission that the man was really struggling with believing his son could be healed. This was more than an admission. It was a cry for help.

"Hall of Faith"

If you didn't know much about football but wondered what it takes to be one of the best players, you would be well served to check out the NFL Hall of Fame in Canton, Ohio. Within its walls, you will see tributes to many of the greatest players ever to don a football uniform. The lengthy list includes such greats as Jim Brown, Jerry Rice, Walter Payton and Joe Namath. In somewhat similar fashion (but certainly infinitely more significant), the Bible has its own "Hall of Faith." We find this charter of heroic patriarchs in Hebrews 11, and among them, the example of Abraham. We will briefly recount his story to see what biblically-commendable faith looks like.

Some quick background to set the stage: God had created a perfect world, but death and a curse entered in because of Adam's sin (Romans 5:12). Fortunately, God had a plan to resolve this problem which involved sending His own Son to die on a cross to pay for the sins of the world (Genesis 3:15, John 3:16, etc.). This also involved choosing a people through which God would bless the entire world. However, humanity had become so corrupt, God destroyed all of mankind except those on the ark (Genesis 6:5-8). After the flood, Noah and his family began repopulating the Earth. It was God's desire that they spread out and fill the Earth, but they refused to do so. Because of this, God confused their language which forced them to move out as He originally intended. At this point, you have a lot of "random people" living all over the planet. It was in this context that God chose one person whose offspring would be His special chosen people and through which the Messiah (His son) would come. Enter Abraham. (Actually, his name was Abram, but later changed to Abraham. We'll simply refer to him as Abraham to keep it simple.)

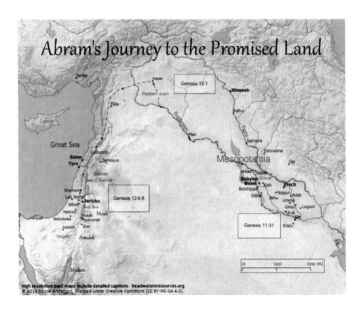

Abraham was living in the land of Ur, which today would be southeastern Iraq. Ur was a fairly pagan area, but God chose Abraham and told him . . .

"Get out of your country, From your family And from your
father's house, To a land that I will show you. I will make
you a great nation; I will bless you And make your name
great; And you shall be a blessing. I will bless those who
bless you, And I will curse him who curses you; And in you
all the families of the earth shall be blessed."
(Genesis 12:1-3).

This blessing included having a son through which the Hebrew
people (aka, the Israelites/Jews) would originate. You are most likely
familiar with Abraham's dilemma. He was no spring chicken and
neither was his wife. At the time of being promised a son, he was
86 and his wife (Sarai, later Sarah) was 77. With this in mind, and
thinking his wife was too old to have children, Abraham thought he
would help God out (never a good idea). He ended up having a son
through Sarah's hand maiden, Hagar. While this was not according
to God's plans, it was culturally acceptable in situations where having
children was not a possibility between a husband and wife.

Fourteen years after the birth of their son, Ishmael, from this union,
Sarah did conceive and gave birth to the son God had promised
Abraham . . . Isaac. At this point, Abraham was 100 and Sarah
was 90!

That was the backdrop for the particular example of faith exercised
by Abraham as referenced in Hebrews 11:17-19. Here's where
Abraham exercised an astonishing amount of faith. God asked him
to sacrifice Isaac, his only son (see further comments later). Abraham
didn't even seem to flinch at this request. He simply reasoned that
since God promised him a son and that through this son the world
would be greatly blessed, then whatever happens, God is able to raise

him from the dead (Heb 1:19). That's great faith! He might have been thinking if Isaac dies, that's not really his problem; that's God's problem and He will have to deal with it.

Some will say it was very strange of God, possibly even "wrong" for Him to ask Abraham to sacrifice his son. Wouldn't that be murder? The focus, interest, and intent by God here is not the potential death of Isaac, but the complete, unquestioning obedience of Abraham. That's an incredible example of faith in action! As an aside, many, when thinking of this story, picture Isaac as a little boy (perhaps grade school age). In reality, he was anywhere from about 20 to 30-year-old, but the Bible doesn't comment enough to be more specific.

Since we're on the subject and not everyone will know this, here are a few additional interesting details about this story.

Many people and events in the Old Testament foreshadow or are "types" of events in the New Testament (or specifically Christ Himself). The story of Abraham and Isaac is a powerful example.

- Both Isaac and Jesus had divinely orchestrated births (Gen 15:16-17 / Matthew 1:23).
- Both are "only sons," as Ishmael was not considered by God to be legitimate (Heb 11:17 / 1 John 4:9).
- Both leave their homeland to be sacrificed (Gen 22:2 / John 6:38).
- Both were led by their fathers (Gen 22:6 / Heb 10:7).
- Both were submissive to their fathers (Heb 22:9 / Heb 10:7).
- Both were sacrificed in the same general area, a mountain in Moriah and Golgotha, respectively (Heb 22:2 / Mark 15:22).
- Both were dead for three days. A note of explanation: Immediately when God asked Abraham to sacrifice his son,

he considered him dead (Heb 11:19). It was a three-day journey to Moriah (Heb 22:4). Once God intervened, Isaac was no longer considered dead. Jesus rose on the third day (1 Cor 15:3-4).

These fascinating facts give us a glimpse of how integral the Old and New Testament are to each other. It is also interesting to note that while ascending the mountain to make the sacrifice, Isaac asks his father, "where is the lamb for the burnt offering?" Abraham didn't respond by saying, "I'm still working on that," or "Got some bad news for you..." Instead, he said, "God Himself will provide the lamb for the burnt offering." That was true back then, when He stopped Abraham in the act and provided a literal lamb (actually, a ram, an equivalent substitute), and it was true 2000 years later when He "provided Himself" (Jesus, God in the flesh) as the "lamb of God that takes away the sins of the world" (John 1:29).

Closing Thoughts

We need to realize that as we live out our faith, we are not doing it through our own strength:

> And my speech and my preaching were not with persuasive words of human wisdom, but in demonstration of the Spirit and of power, that your faith should not be in the wisdom of men but in the power of God (1 Corinthians 2:4-5).

According to this passage, our faith is not based on man's fallible opinions, but on the power of God. Jesus said in Matthew 22:29, "You are in error because you do not know the Scriptures or the power of God." And 1 Corinthians 3:19 states, "For the wisdom of this world is foolishness in God's sight." We certainly don't want to base something as important as our faith on something as tentative and unstable as the limited understanding of men, especially those who reject God and His Word.

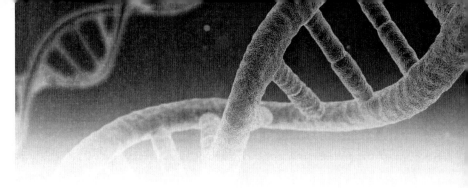

4

Science: What It Is
and What It Ain't

Science Speaks! (Or Not!)

"What did the note say?" someone might ask you. "It didn't *say* anything," comes your reply.

You continue, "It was a piece of paper made from wood pulp, containing strategically placed marks made by graphite within the pencil employed by someone to symbolically convey a specific message using a predetermined system of universally accepted symbols."

"Very funny, Mr. Wise Guy! Just tell me what it said!"

Some of you are laughing. Others are feeling tense because you are forced to deal with things like that on a regular basis. (Sorry, Amy.)

What's the point? Technically speaking, the note really didn't say anything. The person writing it said something. In turn, the reader had to make some initial observations and then offer their opinion as to what they thought they saw. This includes at least two levels of analysis. First, the reader noting what was physically on the paper (i.e., what clearly appeared to be words strung together in a specific sequence). Secondly, the reader doing their best to determine the meaning behind the facts they observed. The second part is critical. It's the "interpretation."

Black & White (Or Not)

Many people have the impression that science is "black & white." It is what it is. Scientists do experiments, the results come out and they just have to live with whatever the evidence says. There's nothing to argue about and those who disagree with the outcome are just being irrational, showing their bias and ignorance. This entire perception, however, is completely false!

Like the note we just described, in reality, facts don't speak for themselves. Every fact you have ever heard or ever will hear, must be interpreted to give it any significant meaning. However, our pre-existing belief system (i.e., our "starting point" or "worldview") will drive how we interpret what we see. We'll touch on that further in chapters 6 and 8.

The word "science" in and of itself has the power to intimidate people. Many are not at all interested in science and many others have some level of fear regarding this potentially technical and complex discipline.

We really need to spend some time figuring out what science actually is and "what it ain't."

The general public often has misguided ideas regarding how science works. One important point to make right off the bat is *science* doesn't really do or say anything... only *scientists* do. We often hear statements claiming that science has proven this or that, but again, science doesn't do or say anything. These claims are simply references to what some scientist (or scientists) said about what they have observed. Science does not speak.

It's not like *science* is this megalithic, all-powerful entity that we must all bow to, but rather it's just an endeavor in which some human beings partake. In other words, science is a specific area of study in which some people engage. It generally consists of having ideas about the physical world, making guesses about things we don't yet know, and then gathering various facts and conducting experiments to see whether or not our initial ideas seem to be very accurate, very inaccurate or somewhere in between.

It is not my intention whatsoever to disparage science in any way, but rather, to reveal its human side and clarify its inherent weaknesses and limitations.

But What Kind of Science?

"I didn't know there were different types of science," you might say.

"You mean the science that Christians do versus the science that skeptics do?" No, not at all.

Much of the intimidation often associated with discussing the creation versus evolution controversy can be removed by simply understanding there are two types of science: operational and historical.

Operational science (sometimes called observational science) deals with things we typically do in a laboratory. It produces cell phones, invents fast computers, and cures diseases, among many, many other things. It's great stuff! Creationists and evolutionists are not debating *operational science*. Both sides know how it works. That's not where the controversy lies. Too often, however, skeptics say, "You creationists; you deny science. You just believe the Bible!" That's not true at all! In fact, most major areas of science were founded by Bible-believing Christians! Want a few examples? Try these:

- Antiseptic Surgery
- Bacteriology
- Calculus
- Chemistry
- Computer Science
- Electronics
- Electrodynamics
- Electromagnetics
- Fluid Mechanics
- Galactic Astronomy
- Gas Dynamics
- Genetics
- Hydraulics
- Hydrostatics
- Oceanography
- Optical Mineralogy
- Optical Mineralogy
- Pathology
- Physical Astronomy
- Stratigraphy
- Thermodynamics
- Thermokenetics
- Vertebrate Paleontology
- Scientific Method

Pretty impressive! Science actually owes its origins to Christianity! It was birthed out of the Christian worldview. So, if you say you don't believe in evolution, you are not saying you don't believe in cell phone technology. One has nothing to do with the other.

The other type of science is known as *historical science*. This deals with events that happened in the past when no one was around to observe them. One example would be belief in the Big Bang. No one was around to see that alleged event happen. We can't repeat it in a laboratory for all to see, and we can't test it directly. However, the same could be said about the Genesis creation account! None of us were around to see that. We certainly can't repeat that in a laboratory, and we can't test it directly. Like the Big Bang, it was a one-time event with no human observers, so they both fall into the category known as *historical science*.

It is very important to note that there is nothing wrong with historical science. It's just different. It involves many guesses and assumptions as to what happened when we weren't there to make any observations. Different scientists have different guesses and assumptions, and that's where the controversy lies. These guesses and assumptions are driven by the individual's personal worldview; their starting point.

The atheist, for example, starts out with the assumption that since the supernatural doesn't exist, whatever happened must have occurred 100% via unguided natural process and probably a very, very long time ago. The Christian actually has an eye-witness account containing a fair amount of detail (i.e., God's Word!). We glean as much as we can from Scripture to further refine our starting point. Then we use the minds God gave us to study His creation, filling in the holes as best we can with the continued guidance of the Holy Spirit. Those are two diametrically opposed approaches, so it's no wonder why each side comes to a starkly different conclusion.

Scientists Are Unbiased (Or Not)

Another misconception regarding science is that scientists in general are unbiased. They simply discover evidence and follow wherever it leads. That sounds very Pollyannaish, at the risk of losing my younger audience. That just means a "pie-in-the-sky" outlook or being "unrealistically optimistic."

As we've been discussing, all data must be interpreted. When we interpret new data based on what we already believe, it's a type of bias. Wouldn't it be better to be unbiased? In some sense, maybe, but it's virtually impossible. And actually, having a bias isn't a bad thing; it's normal. What really matters is admitting what your bias is and being able to offer a reasonable defense for why you've chosen that particular bias. We'll discuss this further throughout this book.

Here's a refreshingly honest example of how bias works from an evolutionist:

> "Nobody looks at a fossil with a completely open mind. I suppose to some extent also we see what we think. So, you come to a fossil and you have an idea about the way you think human evolution worked, and the first thing you do is try and fit that fossil into your worldview."[7]

Here's another very telling admission from Richard Lewontin

(American evolutionary biologist) regarding how one's worldview dictates how they approach science:

> "We take the side of science in spite of the patent absurdity of some of its constructs, in spite of its failure to fulfil many of its extravagant promises of health and life, in spite of the tolerance of the scientific community for unsubstantiated just-so stories, because we have a prior commitment, a commitment to materialism. It is not that the methods and institutions of science somehow compel us to accept a material explanation of the phenomenal world, but, on the contrary, that we are forced by our a priori adherence to material causes to create an apparatus of investigation and a set of concepts that produce material explanations, no matter how counter-intuitive, no matter how mystifying to the uninitiated. Moreover, that materialism is absolute, for we cannot allow a Divine Foot in the door."[8]

Wow! Did you catch that? Simply stated, he will do whatever it takes to come up with natural explanations for everything, no matter how crazy they might sound because he absolutely will not allow God to have any part of the solution! As much as I disagree with his philosophy, I truly appreciate his transparency. I wish there was much more of this honesty in every area of science.

Hijacked the Definition of Science

Occasionally, when someone is having a hard time and they don't like the outcome of whatever they are involved in, they simply change the rules of the game, mid-stream. It may be kind of cute to observe this while watching children playing together, but it's more than a bit disconcerting when it happens in the *real world*, where the effects are significantly more consequential.

The definition of *science* has changed dramatically. In its original state, simply stated, it was:

"Discovering explanations for the natural world around us."

The modified definition looks more like:

"Discovering *natural* explanations for the world around us."

Did you see the subtle change? It might appear subtle on the level of simply examining the words in two juxtaposed sentences, but the meaning change is not subtle at all!

When modern science had its beginnings in the 17th century, it was founded almost exclusively by Christians. Their "starting point" included the belief that it was more than obvious that God supernaturally created everything to begin with. They further reasoned that since God was a God of order, they expected to see order in His creation. They set out to explore the marvelous creation and came upon many regularities. These discoveries served as the basis for many of the scientific laws they formulated, accurately describing the day-to-day operation of life and the universe. Science was focused almost solely on the *operation* of life and the universe, not on the *origin* of these things.

However, some atheistic scientists and philosophers made a *philosophical* decision to change the definition of science to exclude anything not natural, or supernatural. This was extended beyond just discussing how things operate, but also to how EVERYTHING originated.

One of the biggest problems with this is that while the laws of science generally do a very good job of explaining the current *operation* of the world around us, they are totally inadequate when attempting to explain the *origin* of the world around us!

It's kind of like appropriately discussing Boyle's Gas Laws (which deal with compressing and decompressing gases) to explain how your refrigerator operates and then turning around and implying the way we got refrigerators to begin with is simply by compressing and decompressing gases! These laws, which truly do explain the general principle of how a refrigerator functions, are completely inadequate for accounting for the *origin* of refrigerators. The origin required external materials and intelligent engineers designing and coordinating complex manufacturing processes.

What if someone wanted you to explain how the refrigerator was created, but they told you ahead of time, you were not allowed to mention any elements of intelligence. You could only refer to known laws of science? Well, you would be foolish to agree to those terms, and even if you did, you would come up with a pretty crazy story of how gases that came from somewhere became compressed and decompressed and eventually . . . we had refrigerators!

Intimidated by Science

First off, this section should be relabeled as, "Intimidated by Scientists," not "Intimidated by Science." We already discussed that *science* doesn't say or do anything; scientists do.

Here are some of the forms in which intimidation often manifests itself:

1. Overly Technical

Many times the incredible complexity or sheer volume of data can be intimidating. If you don't have the proper training, you won't be able to make heads or tails of what is being presented. A truly good speaker or reporter will take the time to simplify the data so the majority of people will have at least a basic understanding of what is being presented. Even then, you would still have to trust that the presenter is being honest because you are not in an intellectual position to determine truth in this situation for yourself.

Whenever I have heard a lecture and felt like I gleaned very little from the presentation, it is often because the presenter was more interested in impressing the audience with their brilliance than in truly helping them grasp the essentials. Too often, people walk away from a situation such as this saying, "I have no idea what he/she was talking about, but boy, are they smart!"

2. Elephant Hurling

This tactic describes the practice of making many, broad-ranging statements, without giving any evidence of underlying specifics to back up the bold claims being made.

> "When Charles Darwin introduced the theory of Evolution through natural selection 143 years ago, the scientists of the day argued over it fiercely, but the massing evidence from paleontology, genetics, zoology, molecular biology, and other fields gradually established evolution's truth beyond reasonable doubt. Today that battle has been won everywhere—except in the public imagination."[9]

Wow! How could you argue with all the evidence that has been amassed in all those fields of science? Well, you actually could (maybe with some help), if you knew what those evidences actually were, but they didn't mention those details.

I'm certainly not saying you can never make a broad statement such as this. However, it carries no weight until the details are provided. It should not be used as a club to intimidate others, but too often that's exactly what happens. And in our "sound bite society" that's all that is needed to indoctrinate youth and in turn, give them their marching orders. "Believe evolution is a fact of science and repeat this phrase, 'It's been proven by evidence from every area of science!'" So, you have millions of clones walking about chanting this mantra, not really knowing any details behind it. Or more accurately, clones not knowing the actual evidence is greatly lacking!

3. Appeal to Authority

This device relates to referencing a leading authority in some area, with the implication that they must be right because of their high position. It should be more than obvious that those in authority in any area could be wrong, and many times actually are. Arguments must stand on their own merit and not be given a "guaranteed true" status simply because the person making the claim holds a high position in an organization.

4. Shaming

This approach has become more and more popular and powerful. I believe it has become popular solely because it *is* powerful! One of the clearest current examples relates to the COVID-19 pandemic. I am so tired of this whole situation (as are most people) that I hate to mention it because I am perpetuating its memory, even years down the road, by immortalizing it in a book. Hopefully, when you are reading this, you say, "Oh yeah, I think I remember hearing about that. I'm so glad that isn't an issue anymore!" Or you might be saying, "Yes, and here we are in year number 7 of all that pandemonium!"

I realize the pandemic is real and we need to take it seriously. My main frustration has been how the government has been handling it, including removing and greatly restraining our freedoms, many of which we may never regain. I personally do not believe the approach is effective or appropriate. To make things worse, a huge percentage of the general population has bought into the authority's scare tactics. If you are caught not wearing your mask in a situation where technically, it is required, you are often shamed by those around you. Their looks alone say, "You obviously don't care about others! You don't even care if you are the cause of their death!" Unbelievably, virtually all deaths are attributed to those who are questioning authority, even peacefully.

Similar responses are heard regarding climate change. Accusations like, "If you don't submit your will to the climate czars, you obviously don't care about the safety and well-being of others, nor the future of our entire planet!"

5. Eliminate Discussion Possibilities

Getting back to the intimidation of science in general, you are often shouted-down if you dare to disagree with someone else. Your voice is not heard. This eliminates any possible rational dialog. And that's the way they want it! If you are a skeptic, the tactic of only hearing one side is very effective. You can't afford a true, rational debate.

Along these lines, it's interesting to consider something Darwin himself wrote in the Origin of Species:

> "For I am well aware that scarcely a single point is discussed in this volume on which facts cannot be adduced, often apparently leading to conclusions directly opposite to those at which I have arrived. A fair result can be obtained only by fully stating and balancing the facts and arguments on both sides of each question…"[10]

Darwin did not feel he had room in that book to properly cover "both sides," so he made no attempt. This was certainly his prerogative in the context of writing a book. However, when it comes to public policy and other issues, there needs to be room for debate, or it leads to tyranny!

With this in mind, it's interesting to read what Eugenie Scott said regarding teaching both sides of the creation vs evolution controversy within the public-school system. She is the Executive Director of the National Center for Science Education, a group claiming to be religiously neutral but founded by atheists.

> "In my opinion, using creation and evolution as topics for critical-thinking exercises in primary and secondary schools is virtually guaranteed to confuse students about evolution and may lead them to reject one of the major themes in science."[11]

Translation? We can't afford to let the kids hear the best evidence for both views and then decide for themselves! Why that would be akin to teaching them . . . what is it called? Oh, yeah, critical thinking skills!

The following quote from Chinese paleontologist Jun-Yuan Chen is incredibly ironic, especially considering the totalitarian Communistic political environment of her country:

> "In China we can criticize Darwin, but not the government; in America, you can criticize the government, but not Darwin."[12]

6. Settled Science

The concept of "settled science" has been around a long time, but this specific phrase has become more and more common in relation to "global warming" or more specifically "climate change." It can certainly fall under the previous section depicting how  science is used as intimidation, but I decided to treat it separately.

You hear it all the time; "There's no more need for debate. That already happened, and the overwhelming conclusion is that global warming is an undeniable fact! It's not time for debate, it's time for action!"

During the course of a football game, something questionable might occur in one play and the quarterback quickly moves to snap the ball to start the next play before any of the coaches on the opposing team have time to call for a review. It's a very effective move if you can pull it off.

That's what often happens in science, or more accurately, in the political realm. Quickly and emphatically politically motivated individuals claim the research has been done, there's no longer any question, now is the time to implement their policies. They often follow-up with two options, both of which are terrible, and leading conservatives to focus on figuring out how to choose the "lesser of two evils," as opposed to stepping back and saying, "Wait a minute! Why do we have to do either of those?"

I believe we will see more and more of this tactic in the US and globally as we slowly (or not so slowly) move towards one-world government and the rise of the Anti-Christ as depicted in the Bible (Revelation 13:7, *et al*). Yeah, getting off-topic a bit.

7. Consensus Science

We don't determine scientific truth by a democratic vote. Often, all it takes is one discovery for something the majority of scientists had believed for years as being set-in-stone, to suddenly become more like Silly Putty. The intimidation factor arises when someone claims something is obviously true simply because "the majority of scientists believe it!"

After one of my presentations, a Christian university Old Testament professor (who personally believed in evolution) commented, "Of course evolution is a fact. How could all the scientists be wrong?" His point was that it must be true because the majority of scientists believe it. I replied to him with a simple question. "Do you think the majority of scientists believe the Bible is the inspired Word of God?" He emphatically replied, "No!" Then I respectfully inquired, "How could they all be wrong?"

You see, on one hand his logic was to think something must be true because most scientists believe it. However, he was willing to contradict his own logic by admitting that even though the majority of scientists think the Bible is not the inspired Word of God, they are actually wrong!

Here's an interesting comment from a science historian regarding consensus science:

> "Science ... is not so much concerned with truth as it is with consensus. What counts as 'truth' is what scientists can agree to count as truth at any particular moment in time ... [Scientists] are not really receptive or not really open-minded to any sorts of criticisms or any sorts of claims that actually are attacking some of the established parts of the research (traditional) paradigm – in this case neo-Darwinism – so it is very difficult for people who are pushing claims that contradict the paradigm [evolution] to get a hearing. They'll find it difficult to [get] research grants; they'll find it hard to get their research published; they'll, in fact, find it very hard."[13]

8. Academic Censorship

The previous quote provides a great lead-in to the phenomenon of academic censorship. It's somewhat like shouting someone down and not allowing for any debate. It's a "toe our predetermined line or else" attitude. If you are a scientist or a teacher/professor in a secular setting, you better not dare express your doubt in Darwinian evolution, or you'll probably lose your job and your ability to get your work published!

Back in 2008, the American writer, lawyer, and all-around funny guy, Ben Stein, released an excellent documentary entitled, *Expelled: No Intelligence Allowed.* Its focus was not at all on trying to show that evolution is false. And it certainly was not trying to validate the Genesis creation account or even intelligent design. Rather, its primary focus was exposing the fact that if you publicly express doubt in evolution, you're probably toast! He powerfully documented specific examples where this has happened. Numerous more examples could be given now, years after the production of this great work. I highly recommend watching it. For a more thorough discussion of this egregious activity, I recommend a trilogy of books by Dr. Jerry Bergman in which he documents over 100 real-life examples:

1. *Slaughter of the Dissidents* (2011), by Dr. Jerry Bergman.
2. *Silencing the Darwin Skeptics: The War Against Theists* (2016)
3. *Censoring the Darwin Skeptics: How Belief in Evolution Is Enforced by Eliminating Dissidents* (2018).

9. Doggy-Head Tilt

Sometimes you hear things that just make your head tilt. It's not always a bad thing and sometimes can be quite funny. I remember a

time when my family and I were walking
through the atrium of a high-rise office
building where a huge US flag hung
from the ceiling. We overheard a young
girl behind us ask, "Daddy, is that a life-
size flag?" I laughed and could not stop

thinking about her question. To this day, it makes me smile … and
my head still tilts just a bit.

One of my favorite tilt-inducing sayings came from Yogi Berra, a
famous American professional baseball player and coach. Someone
asked whether or not he liked a certain restaurant. He replied, "No,
nobody one goes there anymore. It's too crowded!"

Along the lines of things that make your head tilt, some have
claimed that "creation theory" is not science because it's not testable.
Keep that in mind; it's not testable. Then they turn around and claim
scientists have tested "creation theory" and proven it to be false!
What? How does that work?

In similar fashion, claims have been made that science only deals
with natural processes and cannot comment on anything such as
the supernatural. Then skeptics turn around and claim that science
has disproved the existence of the supernatural. That makes a lot of
sense … if you don't think about it!

Misleading Headlines

If you want to grab someone's attention with a news headline, just
use the phrase, **"This Changes Everything!"** Pretty sensational,

isn't it? Every time I see an article with a similar headline, I tell myself I am going to start tracking these, but then I never get around to it. You could create an entire book with such articles.

Here are a few examples:

Headline: **180,000-year-old human fossil discovery changes what we thought we knew about mankind's history**[14]

Article Snippet: A great deal has happened in recent history that changes everything we thought we knew about the dawn of our species.

Headline: **A handful of recent discoveries have shattered anthropologists' picture of where humans came from, and when**[15]

Article Snippet: Taken together, these breakthroughs suggest that many of our previous ideas about the human origin story — who we are and where we came from — were wrong.

Headline: **JAW DROPPING Fossil found that could change everything we know about the first humans**[16]

Article Snippet: The discovery has led to a re-think of human evolution.

And then from a book:

Book Title: **Evolution Revolution: Evolution is True. Darwin is Wrong. This Changes Everything**[17]

Book Snippet: Neo-Darwinism "is totally wrong… Every major tenet is wrong… It will look ridiculous in retrospect, because it is ridiculous."

I think you get the picture. Let's use a bit of "critical thinking" in relation to the use of the phrase, "This changes everything!" From the first example above, we read, "that changes everything we thought we knew." Using a bit of gray matter, what that means is everything they told us before was wrong!

When we read things in scientific articles or news reports, they are generally portrayed as "fact." Scientists discover something, and now they confidently know whatever it is they are claiming. When they indirectly tell us they were wrong about what they told us before, why should we trust them now? What's different this time?

What if the headlines were all tweaked and basically trumpeted, "We were wrong again!" That wouldn't go over well. You would get tired of seeing it and would trust scientists less and less. It's all marketing!

To make things worse, there is a tacit claim that they are actually right *this* time. But if they were wrong before (and many times over), how do they know they are finally right this time? They don't. So, why don't they say they feel they were definitely wrong in what they previously told us, but now they are strongly leaning towards believing this new idea? That would be much more honest and accurate.

Here's one more example and one of my favorites.

Time Magazine featured a cover story about dinosaurs. They immediately captured almost everyone's attention because it was about dinosaurs and featured a dinosaur picture front and center. Nothing wrong with that. That's effective marketing.

The main title was "THE TRUTH ABOUT DINOSAURS."[18] What can we justifiably assume we will learn if we read their article? Well, it's obvious. They are going to tell us the *truth* about dinosaurs. One might assume Time Magazine would report the truth on all topics without having to make a truth claim. But this truth-headline effectively grabs the reader's attention, assuring editors their audience will purchase their magazine.

And what about the sub-title? This is where it gets even more interesting. When I read the sub-title, my first thought was, "I don't believe they thought that through very deeply." What was the sub-title? Here it is:

Surprise: Just about everything you believe is wrong

Wow! That will serve to grab your attention. Normally, you don't like to find out you are wrong about something. In this case, however, I think most people would be excited and intrigued to find out why they were wrong and what the truth actually is. Critical thinking would take them a slightly different route. They should ask themselves, "Where did I learn most of what I think I know about dinosaurs? Oh yeah, from Time Magazine, Nature, National Geographic, and other secular publications." The reader should realize that if they are wrong about what they currently believe, and what they believe came from the leading secular sources, then the leading secular sources were "wrong about everything" when they reported those things. Hmmm . . .if a source admits their reporting was wrong multiple times before, why should the same source ask its readership to trust them for truth now?

Unfortunately, too many people get caught up in the excitement, thinking, "Wow, they must have discovered something really fascinating and I can't wait to find out what it is. I can tell my friends about this breakthrough, and in a strange way, receive half the credit for these discoveries myself."

Another Pseudo-Truth Twist on Headlines

Headlines can have another powerful detrimental effect. It has to do with the direct or indirect claims within the headline, not being supported by anything in the actual article.

Try this headline on for size:

New light shed on Charles Darwin's 'abominable mystery'[19]

Let's think this through. What do you suppose the initial reaction is in most people's mind when they see a headline like this? I think the vast majority would get the impression that whatever the mystery was that Darwin was referring to, scientists have discovered something that helps us better understand what the solution is. That's certainly what I would think, and I believe that's what the article's author hopes people will think.

What was the mystery being referenced? Charles Darwin really struggled figuring out the origin of flowering plants. He called it an "abominable mystery." In case you are not familiar with the word "abominable," it means repulsive, offensive, detestable, etc. It really bothered Darwin. Why?

In a letter written in 1879 to his good friend, Dr. Joseph Hooker, Darwin quoted Professor Richard Buggs, Professor of Evolutionary Genomics at the Queen Mary University of London:[20]

> "The rapid development as far as we can judge of all the higher plants within recent geological times is an abominable mystery. In the fossil record they appear very suddenly in the Cretaceous... and there's nothing that looks like an angiosperm [flowering plant] before them and then they suddenly appear and in considerable diversity."

Guess what? Scientists aren't any closer to solving this problem! The BBC article ends by admitting this is still a mystery:

> "One hundred and forty years later, the mystery's still unsolved," says Prof Buggs. "Of course, we've made lots of progress in our understanding of evolution and in our knowledge of the fossil record, but this mystery is still there."

Here's where the article headline and the article itself becomes a problem. The majority of people will only read the headline and never get around to reading the actual article. So, they walk away with the impression that once again, scientists have discovered further evidence for evolution. In their minds, the evidence just keeps piling up, and therefore, they would be foolish to deny evolution!

Others will see the headline and start to the read the article, but not get very far. They, too, generally espouse the same conclusion as those who didn't read any of the article, but only saw the headline.

Still others will read the entire article and feel that there was nothing all that exciting revealed, nothing very memorable, yet still walk away concluding the same pseudo truth the headline implies.

Very, very few people read the entire article and rightly conclude: "Wait a minute! There's really no new light shed on Darwin's dilemma. No evidence for evolution was presented. No solution to the problem was offered. What were they talking about? They didn't deliver on what their headline intimates they would cover."

This may seem like a minor example, and in some respects it is. However, when you multiply this by hundreds of examples, year after year, its effect becomes extremely significant, and a huge reason for concern. This especially holds true in light of the fact that as a culture, we have lost our critical thinking abilities.

In the next chapter, we will examine examples of when "science" was wrong. Very interesting, revealing and insightful.

5

When Science Gets It Wrong!

When Science Gets It Wrong!

$\mathcal{B}$ecause many people equate "science" with "scientists' opinions," I use this heading in a general sense. But what I really mean by this heading is, "When *Scientists* Get It Wrong."

The following examples provide hard evidence of how unreliable "consensus science," (the idea that truth is determined by majority opinion) truly is. These historical incidents remind us of times when the majority opinion turned out to be completely false.

Wash Your Hands!

One of my dad's nicknames was "Mr. Clean." Some of you may remember that name from old television commercials. My dad was

very big on washing his hands
frequently and getting you to wash
yours, too.

This first example of a time when
"science got it wrong" (i.e., the
majority were staunchly wrong)

concerns a Hungarian medical doctor named Ignaz Semmelweis
(1818-1865).[21] His entire story is fascinating, but here, I only
summarize it. Mortality rates in Europe for women giving birth in
hospitals was 25-30%. That means 25-30% of those women were
dying subsequent to giving birth! That's a horrible statistic.

Any death is tragic, but consider the following, which is not intended
to be an apples-to-apples comparison. Think about the extreme
response reaction we experienced related to the COVID-19 virus
death rate (2020-2021) which was incredibly low; only 0.050%.
[World Health Organization: (Totals deaths: 3.93 Million, Total
Population: 7.8 Billion)[22] If scientists in the 1800s were anywhere
close to being as concerned about mortality rates of their day as
modern scientist apparently are about COVID, they would have
wasted no time and moved heaven and Earth to resolve the issue they
were facing. In reality, they resisted solutions, as we shall see next.

Semmelweis observed a connection related to doctors who were
doing an autopsy in one room, then without cleaning up, walking
across the hall to assist in delivery of a new born baby. He started
washing in water and chlorine and noticed a dramatic drop in
deaths. He urged the other doctors to do the same but was met
with ridicule and hostility. They felt the idea was silly, and maybe
more significantly, Semmelweis was implicating them as the main

cause of all the deaths! His practice at the Vienna General Hospital expired and they refused to renew it. In his next position (St Rochus Hospital, Pest, Hungary) he reduced the mortality rate to 0.85%! Amazing! Still, he was getting responses such as this one from the Viennese Medical Weekly, "It was time to stop the nonsense about chlorine hand wash."

Fast-forwarding a bit when in 1865, against his will, he was interned in a mental hospital. When he tried to escape, he was beaten severely by the guards and died two weeks later at the young age of 47!

It would be decades later that his ideas would finally be put into regular practice. How tragic! This is just one example of very serious consequences related to the views of the vast majority overpowering truth!

Junk DNA

Although many people attribute the discovery of DNA to Watson and Crick in the 1950s, it was actually discovered much earlier in 1869 by Swiss-born biochemist Fredrich Miescher. Watson and Crick (and others) conducted further experiments leading to the discovery of its double-helix structure.

The more DNA has been studied, the more complex it appears to be. (See our video series entitled, *Evolution: Probable or Problematic?*[23]) Along the way, it seemed that only 2% of our DNA did anything (i.e., coded to make proteins that carry out most of the functions in our bodies). The other 98% appeared to be useless junk. Secular scientists assumed this was due to DNA's evolutionary development and used this statistic as strong evidence against intelligent design. What kind of Intelligent Designer would create something that is 98% junk? Hence, the term "junk DNA" was born.

Subsequent to this determination, further research has been conducted. What secular scientists thought to be "junk" turned out not only to be useful, but more complex than the 2% that makes proteins! In a simplified summary, the 98% consists of complex instructions that tell the 2% how to do its job!

Here's an interesting admission from Professor John Mattick (University of Queensland in Brisbane, Australia):

> "The failure to recognize the implications of the non-coding ["junk"] DNA will go down as the biggest mistake in the history of molecular biology."[24]

It was actually the scientists' "starting point" or worldview (i.e., belief in Darwinian evolution) that lead them to draw the errant conclusion to begin with. Creationists were saying, "Let's keep researching, because we believe DNA was designed by God, so there should be a purpose for the large portion of DNA we don't yet fully understand."

Plates of the Earth

I don't know if you've ever noticed, but the geological plates of the Earth are big, really big! From the inception of modern science and for many years following, the general view was that the plates of the Earth are static. They don't move. That was the scientific consensus.

In 1859, two significant ideas were put forth. The first is one that everyone is at least somewhat familiar with. That would be the publication of Darwin's *Origin of Species*, greatly promoting and expounding on the idea of evolution, which had been around for quite a while, but was never widely popularized or accepted. The second idea was that of the movement of the Earth's plates. This was proposed by Antonio Snider-Pellegrini, a Christian geographer. His book, *The Creation and Its Mysteries Unveiled* (English equivalence of the French title), presented his theory that the Earth's plates were originally together but were torn apart during the Genesis flood.

His ideas were largely ignored, partially due to all the attention given to Darwin's book and its controversial nature. A little over five decades later in 1912, German scientist Alfred Wegener proposed a similar idea, but claimed the plates gradually moved apart. His views were also rejected, primarily because he did not offer a mechanism to account for such phenomenon.

It wasn't until the 1960s that the concept of continental drift gained popularity and is now accepted by virtually all scientists. More specifically, they agree the continents were together in the past and have moved apart. The major difference in their opinions is the amount of time the separation has taken. Both secular scientists and also many religious scientists believe the separation happened slowly over millions and millions of years. However, scientists who believe in a literal six-day creation as depicted in Genesis 1-2 conclude the plates moved catastrophically during the Genesis flood. Those who believe in the concept of millions and billions of years of Earth history and that the plate separation took massive time periods still lack a valid mechanism for their model. On the other hand, six-day creationists have a very powerful model called "catastrophic plate tectonics," initially put forth by Dr. John Baumgardner, PhD Geophysicist. I am on the Board of Directors for Logos Research Associates along with Dr. Baumgardner. He developed the world's best 3-D computer simulation of plate tectonics and it is used by secular scientists today to predict future movement.

Once again, this offers another example of where the majority was wrong, and in this case, for over 100 years!

Y2K

This is one I can relate to because it involves the computer industry. I was a computer programmer for 12 years and even had my own consulting business for 5 of those years. Some of you remember the Y2K global threat quite clearly. For those of you who don't, here's the skinny.

Because of how they were designed, computers only used 2 digits to determine the year of any particular date. For instance, June 3, 1997 (my daughter's birthday!) was recorded as "06/03/97." We're all familiar with that format because we use it regularly in our daily lives. Here's the problem. What date is this: 06/03/05? You say, "That's June 3, 2005." How do you know it's not June 3, 1905? Or even 1805 or 1705, etc.? You don't know! Up to the time of this crisis, computers were assuming all the dates were in the 1900s! Talk about being short-sighted!

When we approached the year 2000, there were concerns that all the computer systems would see "01/01/00" as January 1, 1900! That could wreak havoc. There was talk of planes falling out of the sky, banking systems collapsing, patients in hospitals dying. It was potentially the end if the world in the minds of many people. No one really seemed to know for sure. We ended up spending about $100 billion to *fix* a problem we had not verified would truly be a problem.

If you are wondering how it all ended, here's what happened. The Earth did blow up, but we all escaped to this planet on the giant Space Ark. What, you don't remember that? Really? You don't remember? Yes, we all escaped on the Space Ark and the government decided not to tell the less educated people because… Oooooh, never mind. Sorry, that was something I heard from a Steve Martin comedy routine when I was in high school. Forgive me for the childish rabbit trail, but I had to fit that humor in somewhere.

In reality, it turned out to be nothing of any real significance. Now we just have to worry about the year 10,000 and I don't think we'll be around that long!

And if That Wasn't Enough…

Dishonesty Within the Scientific Community

This is an entire category unto itself, but it plays a very significant role regarding blindly trusting whatever comes out of the scientific community.

There are numerous examples of scientists being very dishonest about their research and/or their findings. This reproach can be driven by personal gain, political biases, peer pressure, or a number of other factors. I will list just one example, that at the time of writing, is a very significant issue.

In an attempt to combat the COVID-19 disease, scientists have been working on various vaccines. Simultaneously, many doctors have been promoting the use of hydroxychloroquine, 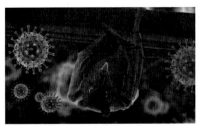 a prescription drug developed in the 1940s, first used to treat malaria. I will refrain from political commentary but use of this "over-the-counter" drug to treat COVID-19 patients posed a huge financial threat to those largely invested in the promotion of unvetted expensive treatments and vaccines.

In an effort to dissuade people from pursuing the use of hydroxychloroquine, the CDC (Center for Disease Control) claimed a study had been conducted of 96,000 COVID-19 patients from 671 hospitals on five continents who were treated with hydroxychloroquine. The article was published in *The Lancet* (the world's leading medical journal) and claimed hydroxychloroquine did not help curb COVID-19 and might even cause death in patients.

The problem? No one seemed to be familiar with the study, even leading doctors. When asked for verification of this study, *The Lancet*, under pressure, admitted they were unable to provide such information and agreed to retract the article. Too late! The damage had already been done! It was a cover story and the message had already gone viral. The subsequent retraction did not enjoy such fanfare, as you can well imagine!

Many Other Examples

There are voluminous examples of these types of occurrences, but I think you get the point. So you don't misunderstand, I am certainly not faulting science simply because theories have to be tweaked and corrected. That's just the nature of science. It's a built-in feature. We can't get around it, and it's completely understandable. What I am pointing out is there are many times when the majority of scientists believe something, and pressure is placed on the masses to accept it as accurate . . . at least until the same majority change their mind. We should learn an important lesson from all of this.

Hopefully you now have a better understanding of what science is all about, especially the difference between *operational* science and *historical* science. This should serve to remove some of the intimidation from scientific academia as well.

6

Ultimate Authority

When you break it down to its most fundamental level, Christianity consists of two major elements. The belief that (a) God exists and (b) you're not Him! Actually, that's just another example of my dry sense of humor. The second fundamental is that the Bible is the inspired Word of God. So, the two major elements are: God exists, and the Bible is God's Word. These are also the two fundaments elements of our starting point as Christians.

Ultimate Authority

When you think of the existence of God, I'm sure the first thing that comes to mind is a coil of rope, right? Maybe not, but it's a very useful analogy.Let's say you went to a hardware store and informed one of the employees that you needed one meter of rope.

The assistant walks over to the coil, cuts a piece off, hands it to you and says, "There you go!" You then ask, "But how do I know it's one meter?" The assistant says, "I know it's a meter because I used a tape measure." At this point, he or she is appealing to a "higher authority." It's not just someone's opinion or best guess; they're using a tape measure, a higher authority. If you were inclined for some reason to give this assistant a bit of a hard time, you might ask, "But how do I know the tape measure is accurate?" They might respond by telling you

they know it's correct because these tape measures are manufactured in a very high-tech plant. They are now appealing to an even higher authority, the manufacturing plant. Now, if you were in a particularly feisty mood, you might also ask, "But how do I know they do it right in the manufacturing plant?" If the assistant doesn't call the manager over and have you kicked out, they might say, "Well, I know they're doing it correctly in the manufacturing plant because they are using the standards that were established at the General Conference on Weights and Measures in 1983 during which they decided that a meter was going to be the distance light traveled in a vacuum in one 299,792,458th of a second!" That's extremely precise! In essence, this conference serves not just as a higher authority, but actually as the "ultimate authority" on how long a meter is. It's the end of the line. There's no appealing to a higher authority. A meter happens to be this length because they say it is. End of story!

This is a fairly simple analogy, but I think you get the picture. The employee appealed to a higher authority until he got to the highest or ultimate authority. At that point, you can't appeal to anything higher to verify whatever it is you are considering. It's the end of the line. It can't go on forever and ever... it's got to stop somewhere. With this logic in mind, consider the following.

If the Bible truly is the Word of God, then for Christians, it must be our ultimate authority. However, if it is our ultimate authority, then we don't try to prove God's existence and the inspiration of the Bible in a traditional manner. Here's why. In using a traditional approach, we would need to appeal to an even higher authority (as in the rope analogy), but in this case, a higher authority does not exist. It's not as if there exists some "mega-god" who happens to be "bigger and better" than our God and we appeal to this mega-god to confirm that the Bible we trust was actually inspired by the lessor God that we worship. You can't go any higher than the God of the Bible.

So, we don't use a traditional approach to "prove" the Bible is from God. Rather, we hold these beliefs (the existence of God and the inspiration of the Bible) as our starting point and then subsequently demonstrate that without accepting these core beliefs, it is actually impossible to rationally know or "prove" anything else.

Is your head spinning yet? If not, maybe you could re-read the previous section. I know this is a bit tricky, but it's a very important concept, so I would suggest turning to Appendix A for further details.

Can't Get There from Here

The humorous story is told of a man looking for a special restaurant but was unable to find it. He pulled into a gas station to ask for directions. The attendant said, "Oh, if that's where you want to go, you don't want to start from here." You may be rolling your eyes, but that's my kind of humor. What's the connection with this book? Starting points are important, they constitute our worldview and they drive the meaning of everything else we think about.

Everyone has a foundation for their belief system or worldview. That is, everyone has to start somewhere with their beliefs. It's impossible not to. There's no avoiding it. We call these ideas our "starting points," our "bias," our "presuppositions," or our "beginning assumptions." These "starting points," while not being proven using traditional methods, do need to be self-authenticating, as opposed to self-contradictory. Again, see Appendix A for further explanation.

The Skeptic's Foundation

The skeptic would like you to think that the foundation for everything they believe consists of facts, whereas the Christian's foundation is all blind faith. I am going to show you a hypothetical conversation that you might have with this skeptic. Please keep in mind, that for the context of this conversation, when I mention "science" I am not referring to "operational science" which mainly deals with things we can directly test in a laboratory over and over. What I am referring to is "historical science" which deals with events that happened in the distant past when we were not around to observe. See chapter 4 for further discussion of this very important difference.

Here's the potential conversation:

You: "What's your foundation,
            everything you believe?"

Skeptic: "Facts!"

You: "What do you mean by 'facts'?"

Skeptic: "You know, science and proving things."

You: "But what is 'science'? It largely consists of the thoughts
            and opinions of various men and women around
            the world. They consider certain historically related
            questions (such as the origin of the universe and life) and
            tell us what they think. How do you know you can trust
            the thoughts and opinions of other men and women, the
            vast majority of which you've never even met?"

Skeptic: "Well, I can think about what they are saying, and
            I can tell they're right because what they are saying
            makes sense."

You: "Ok. So, you're using your reasoning to figure out
            whether or not they are correct."

Skeptic: "Yes."

You: "How do you know you can trust your reasoning?"

Skeptic: "Well, I know I can trust it because it's consistently worked for me my entire life."

You: "OK. So, now you're using your reasoning to justify
                whether or not you can trust your reasoning. That's
                something called 'circular reasoning'. But that's
                actually alright because you have to start somewhere.
                I just wanted you to realize that although you initially
                claimed your foundation was based solely on 'facts,' your
                true foundation is that you ultimately trust your own
                reasoning, but you can't actually prove that it's reliable;
                not without using your reasoning in the process. I'm
                not saying that can't be your starting point. I just
                wanted you to better understand what it really means."

The Christian's Foundation

We just took a closer look at what the skeptic's ultimate foundation
is. How about the Christian? What is our ultimate foundation?
What is our starting point? Let's rejoin our conversation to find out.

Skeptic: "OK, mister wise guy, what is your starting point?"

You: "I believe that God exists, and the Bible is the Word
                of God."

Skeptic: "You can't prove that!"

You: "Actually, this belief proves itself, when analyzed
                internally, whereas your choice of a starting point
                cannot stand up to internal scrutiny. Everyone has to

start somewhere. You picked what you wanted for your starting point and I picked mine. And my starting point is that I believe that God exists, and the Bible is the Word of God. I can actually demonstrate these beliefs are internally consistent and true, whereas you cannot demonstrate objectively that your starting point is valid."

Summary

We've just briefly analyzed the foundational content that typically makes up the skeptic's "starting point."

Our goal is to demonstrate that their starting point is self-contradictory and self-defeating, as opposed to self-consistent and self-authenticating. We are helping the skeptic to understand:

1. They actually do have a starting point, whether they realized it or not, and
2. If their starting point is fraught with internal problems, it will not serve them well when they use it to define everything else going forward.

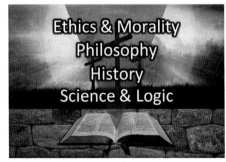

So, the Christian begins by believing that God exists, and the Bible is His inspired Word. We then build our understanding of everything else upon this foundation, including our ideas regarding science, logic, history, philosophy, ethics, and morality. This makes perfect sense because the Bible is our ultimate authority.

This will make more and more sense as we delve further into the details. Be patient.

In the next chapter we'll discuss some helpful advice on sharing our faith!

7

The Suggested Approach

Witnessing to Skeptics

So, how do we approach witnessing to skeptics? My advice is to start where we as Christians start for ourselves; with our "starting point." If belief in God and the Bible being His inspired Word is our "starting point" as Christians, then we should really start there when approaching skeptics. But the skeptic doesn't believe the Bible and they often say, "You have to leave the Bible out of this!" Let's think about this for a second.

When someone says, "You need to leave the Bible out of this," too often the Christian capitulates and proceeds with the conversation apart from mentioning Scripture. Warning! As soon you agree to this request (or demand), you've lost. You're toast. One reason is that you are not there to argue your philosophy against theirs. You are there to share the claims of the Bible and to discuss their response to those claims. When you "leave the Bible out of it," you make it all about yourself. At this point, who are you that the whole world should care what you have to say about anything? You are just one voice amongst about 8 billion others.

More importantly, you've just given up your "starting point," your foundation. How can you possibly be successful when you have no foundation to stand upon? Here's something very important most Christians don't realize about this situation. When a skeptic says, "You have to leave the Bible out of this!" they are implicitly saying, "You have to give up your starting point!" Guess what? They are not giving up theirs. You both come into the discussion with beliefs. You believe the Bible *is* the inspired Word of God. They believe the Bible *is NOT* the inspired Word of God. They want you to leave your view of the Bible out, but they keep theirs. How in the world can this ever be an effective conversation?

Let's say you were at an old western gun fight and, unfortunately, you are one of the two participants. Imagine the other fighter telling you that you need to leave your gun out of this! You would never agree to that completely unreasonable request. You would also understand that if you did indeed comply, you would have already lost. You wouldn't stand a chance!

So, why would you agree to giving up your view of the Bible if requested to do so? A much better response would be to say something like, "We both are coming into this conversation with beliefs about the world in which we live. Instead of giving up those beliefs and then trying to have a meaningful discussion, why don't we simply admit what those beliefs are and then offer a defense along the way? If our beliefs are not at all defensible, it will probably be pretty apparent."

One caveat to all of this . . . I believe the most effective way to share our faith is to first establish a relationship with someone. If at all possible, spend some time just being a friend, establishing some rapport with them to the point where they enjoy talking with you and respect who you are as a person. This involves listening to them, offering assistance with anything you are able to help them with, caring, being kind and patient. Who wouldn't want to be around that kind of person? When the opportunity arises for you to share more specifically about your biblical views, you will have "earned" the right to convey your thoughts and ideas on life's most basic and important issues like how we got here, why we are here and what happens to us when we die. Obviously, we are not always able to develop this relationship. In this scenario, we trust the Holy Spirit as much as in any other situation and tactfully jump right in.

When you do approach a skeptic, I highly recommend that you do the following three things:

1. Pray about it.
2. Share what the Bible says.
3. Share why you believe the Bible is the Word of God.

Let's look at each of these briefly.

Pray About It

Since someone's conversion to Christ is ultimately a spiritual matter,

one driven by the drawing of
the Holy Spirit, we should not
enter into these conversations
or confrontations alone, relying
on our own wisdom and
strength. We want to ask God
to prepare their heart ahead of
time and to help us be open to
God's leading in how and what we share.

There have been numerous occasions where I ended up sharing something that I had no intention of even mentioning heading into the conversation. Later I found out that it was incredibly powerful because of some detail of which I was completely unaware. It was very clear to me afterwards that the Holy Spirit was strongly guiding and directing at that time. I've also experienced times when I thought of something I forgot to mention and was initially very frustrated because I felt it was a particularly powerful point. However, later when I learned more about the person I was speaking to, I realized God was purposely allowing (or causing) me to skip that point because it would have had a strong negative affect on the conversation. There are many times when I included something out of the ordinary or forget something that is routinely part of my talk, and never did figure out exactly why. But God has taught me to trust that ultimately He was in control and He will use what I say when I follow His leading.

The importance of prayer cannot be understated. We don't want to enter into evangelistic opportunities simply using our own wisdom. Here are a few verses discussing the importance of prayer in general:

Likewise the Spirit also helps in our weaknesses. For we do not know what we should pray for as we ought, but the Spirit Himself makes intercession for us with groanings which cannot be uttered (Romans 8:26).

Be anxious for nothing, but in everything by prayer and supplication, with thanksgiving, let your requests be made known to God; and the peace of God, which surpasses all understanding, will guard your hearts and minds through Christ Jesus (Philippians 4:6-7).

If any of you lacks wisdom, let him ask of God, who gives to all liberally and without reproach, and it will be given to him (James 1:5).

Share What the Bible Says

What do I mean by this? All too often we just assume the skeptic generally knows what the Bible teaches, and we simply set out to "prove" to them that it is correct (or directly inspired by God). There's a problem with this approach and I have been guilty of this too many times in the past. I have spent countless hours trying to convince people that the Bible truly is the inspired Word of God and in a number of instances, it worked. They were actually convinced. The problem, however, is I didn't really spend any significant time sharing *what* the Bible teaches about God, forgetting that most skeptics have a fairly warped view of God.

I venture to say that most skeptics view God as a mean ogre who hates them and who is just waiting for them to mess up one more time.

Then, BOOM! God will severely punish them for whatever they did and eventually send them to hell. Most unbelievers also have the impression that they have to try very hard to be good enough in order to be accepted by God. Then I come along and say, "Yes, the Bible is true!" and they now feel their (misguided) ideas about God are true as well. How depressing that must be for them to hear. No wonder they don't what to believe in my God and His Written Word!

So do not assume the skeptic accurately understands the Bible's real message. Most skeptics have never read the Bible and their opinion of the Bible is based on what someone else told them. The skeptic's view of the Bible usually stands in stark contrast to what it truly teaches. Before we focus on defending why we believe in the inspiration of God's Word, we need to share what it actually says about God and what is says about our relationship to Him. I suggest at least briefly covering the following major points:

1. God created the entire universe, including us, mankind. (Jeremiah 32:17, Genesis 2:7)
2. Mankind chose to disobey God and was separated from God because of our sin. (Genesis 3)
3. Man's sin brought death and a curse into God's perfect creation. Every individual is born a sinner and chooses to sin, failing to meet God's standard of 100% holiness. (Romans 5:12, 19a)
4. God did not want man to be eternally separated from him, so He made a plan to send His own son, Jesus to die on a cross for the sins of the world. (Genesis 3:15 – *first reference to the solution*, John 3:16 – *fulfillment*)
5. Our salvation is achieved not by us working hard and trying

to be good enough, but solely by placing our faith in the death and resurrection of Jesus, who paid for our sins, once and for all. (Galatians 2:16)

6. Jesus is the only way to God and to heaven. (John 14:6)

Share why you believe in God and the Bible is the Word of God

Suppose you just returned from the vacation of a lifetime. It was a place you'd never been before, and it was absolutely amazing! Now imagine a stranger tells you they are thinking about planning a vacation. They want to have a great experience, but they've been burned a few times in the past and they aren't sure where to go. Then you tell them to go to such-and-such a place (where you just visited). They ask why you think that's where they should go and you reply, "You should just go because I went there." Would that be a very powerful and effective recommendation? Not at all.

You would probably appear visibly excited and offer a glowing, hard-to-argue-with justification as to why that should be their choice of locations. You would probably share a fair amount of detail, such as cost of airfare, accommodation options, excursions available, wonderful restaurant choices, valet service, and on and on. They may say something like, "What, are you a travel agent or something? Do you get a commission if we go there?"

How much more effort should you put into sharing your faith?

You should be visibly energized and be able to share an impressive list of reasons why you believe what you believe, including what a difference it has made in your own life. You don't always have time to do it justice, but you should at least be prepared to share why you are confident that God exists and that the Bible is actually His inspired Word. If you think about it, if you can't somewhat adequately offer responses to those two most basic beliefs, why would someone listen to anything else you had to say?

The Groundwork Has Been Laid

Shocker alert! The atheist already knows God exists! That should certainly help when talking with them. Wait a minute, atheists don't believe in God, so how can that be? I will cover that further in the next chapter, so put that one on hold for the moment. It's very interesting and pretty straight-forward. You'll also be learning a solid defense for the existence of God.

When we don't provide persuasive reasons, we offer nothing more than a blind faith and the plea to "try it out; it worked for me." Well, Mormonism works (to a certain extent) for Mormons, so why not give that one a try as well? Or how about Hinduism? In fact, why not try all religious systems and see which is the best or at least which works best for you? No, it's not about urging someone to *try Christianity* and see how it goes. It's about accurately explaining the Christian worldview, offering a powerful defense for why we believe in the Divine inspiration of the Bible, and then allowing the Holy Spirit to do all the "heavy lifting" to bring clarity and conviction to the skeptic's heart.

As we continue learning about reaching the skeptic's heart, there are more tools we can employ. In the next three chapters, we will look at how we use evidence while sharing and examining the Christian worldview.

8

Evidence Is Not Proof

The Christian faith is unquestionably founded upon actual historical events. That means you can conduct investigations into its historical roots. Among the most prominent elements is the resurrection of Christ. It is not the intent of this book to launch into an apologetic for this event, but much evidence has been amassed and the case for the reality of the resurrection is astounding!

A typical defense of Christianity as a whole would involve looking at the complexities of DNA (in support of a purposeful Creator as opposed to undirected forces of nature), discussing evidence for the resurrection of Jesus, and examining Greek and Hebrew manuscripts verifying the authenticity and accuracy of the Old and New Testament. I have spent over 35 years sharing fascinating, faith-building details in these areas with countless people.

However, we should not be trying to use evidence as "proof." Especially early on in my apologetics career, I had been guilty of doing just that . . . claiming this or that "proves" the Bible is correct, that the creation account is accurate, and that God exists. I was very well intentioned, as are most others who have done the same or who are currently doing so, but I also feel that I was unintentionally missing the mark. Like many other ventures, defending the faith is a maturing process. Our gracious God still uses our feeble efforts all along the way. One reason I am so thankful for this is that not only did God use my imperfect efforts in the past to His glory, He's still doing it today even as I write this book. I will never have "arrived," but it certainly has been an enjoyable, exciting journey. The more God refines me, the more I get to know who He really is and the more I realize just how gracious He is towards me!

So, why shouldn't we use evidence as proof? We'll get to that next.

What Constitutes Proof?

The word "proof" is used in many ways. When we are discussing evolution with people, we need to define our terms to make sure we are on the same page. The same holds true when speaking about "proof." It can be exhausting to have a conversation or a debate with someone when you are unknowingly talking about two different things. You'll probably just end up spinning your wheels and getting frustrated.

We use the word "proof" loosely at times, such as when we might glibly say football is proof God loves us. (I guess you can figure out pretty easily what sport I like best.) In a courtroom situation, they often refer to "*prima facie*" evidence. *Prima facie* is Latin for "on its first encounter or at first sight." According to Cornell Law School, the legal definition of *prima facie* means, "sufficient to establish a fact or raise a presumption unless disproved or rebutted."

This type of evidence holds true when virtually all other options have been ruled-out. In one sense, this constitutes a form of "proof." This type of proof works well when there are no direct eyewitnesses. Here's a simple example.

Let's say your next-door neighbor lives in an igloo. (I know, work with me here.) It has no windows and only one entrance leading to one large open room inside. You happen to be in this unique home visiting with the single man who lives there and no one else is with you. You finish your conversation and walk out the front door which is the only entrance and exit.

As you are walking away, you see a masked man holding a gun in his hand running up to the neighbor's igloo and in through the only entrance. Seconds later you hear five shots fired and then you see the masked man running out of the house with the smoking gun in his hand. You quickly hurry back over to your neighbor's igloo to find that he has been shot five times and is dead. Later, the medical examiner determines your neighbor was shot from about 10 feet away and died from the bullet wounds. The masked man is quickly apprehended and the bullets at the scene match his gun which also shows evidence of recently having been fired five times.

If this were to go to court, do you think the masked man would be convicted of murder? Most people would unhesitatingly say "Yes, of course!" However, no one saw the crime, so how can there be a conviction? Because there is a *prima facie* case; all other possibilities can be justifiably ruled out. So, in this case, most people would be comfortable consenting that the prosecution demonstrated "proof" as to who the murderer was.

Within the realm of science, we can never say with assurance that no future discoveries will overturn what we deem today as being true. Even though there might be a high level of confidence in many cases because finding something to the contrary seems so incredibly remote and against everything we currently know; there's never really any finality.

This reality is confirmed by a letter signed by 255 members of the U.S. National Academy of Sciences:

> "All citizens should understand some basic scientific facts. There is always some uncertainty associated with scientific conclusions; science never absolutely proves anything."[25]

In chapter 4 we discussed what science is, including how it can be used to intimidate people. I might be reading more into this quote than others, but it contains a subtle level of intimidation in the form of condescension. "All citizens should know . . ." comes from elitist scientists living in their lofty towers. They are graciously taking time out of their day to educate the great unwashed masses living in the underworld who don't, and probably can't, understand science. I can picture someone standing out on a balcony holding a bullhorn addressing a huge crowd below, pontificating, "Citizens of the world, please listen to me. I have something very important to say . . ." Sorry, I'm getting wound up here, but it does reiterate the intimidation concepts we looked at in chapter 4 and often overlook in this type of haughty scientific dialogue.

In summary, because it's impossible to prove there will never be any contravening discovery in the future, we can never say that any particular scientific conclusion is an absolute fact. In many cases, it may appear extremely unlikely that there are other possibilities, so we view whatever is under consideration as being a "virtual fact."

Lest you think all of this is simply my opinion, here's a telling quote from Evolutionary Psychologist, Satoshi Kanazawa.

> "One of the most common misconceptions concerns the so-called 'scientific proofs.' Contrary to popular belief, there is no such thing as a scientific proof... all scientific knowledge is tentative and provisional, and nothing is final. There is no such thing as final proven knowledge in science. The currently accepted theory of a phenomenon is simply the best explanation for it among all available alternatives. Its status as the accepted theory is contingent on what other theories are available and might suddenly change tomorrow if there appears a better theory or new evidence that might challenge the accepted theory. No knowledge or theory (which embodies scientific knowledge) is final... The creationists and other critics of evolution are absolutely correct when they point out that evolution is 'just a theory' and it is not 'proven.'"[26]

Even an institution as liberal as UC Berkeley confirms this scientific uncertainty in their writing about "Misconceptions about science":

MISCONCEPTION: Science proves ideas.

CORRECTION: Journalists often write about "scientific proof" and some scientists talk about it, but in fact, the concept of proof — real, absolute proof — is not particularly scientific. Science is based on the principle that any idea, no matter how widely accepted today, could be overturned tomorrow if the evidence warranted it. Science accepts or rejects ideas based on the evidence; it does not prove or disprove them.[27]

I'll wind this sub-section down with an important point to keep in mind. The fact that evidence does not equate proof is certainly not a limitation unique to the Christian worldview. It is an inherent truth for any given topic, any worldview. I mention this to ensure no one sees this as being a weakness with Christianity or our faith. It holds true no matter what subject you might be discussing.

With that limitation defined, let's take a look at specific problems when trying to use evidence as proof.

Seven Reasons Not to Use Evidence as Proof

1. People Interpret the Facts Differently

You may be too young to remember the old black and white television show, "Dragnet," which featured Jack Web as a detective. He was famous for saying, "Just the facts, ma'am."

Contrary to popular belief, however, facts do not speak for

themselves. Every fact you've ever heard or will ever hear, needs to be interpreted to give it any kind of meaning. The problem is that we use our bias or worldview to determine our interpretation, and we generally come up with an interpretation that agrees with our worldview (i.e., what we already believe).

Let's look at a real-life example — DNA.

A Christian would look at the immense complexity and intricacy of DNA and claim that this is "proof" that God created it. After all, there's no way this could have evolved by accident.

An atheist might look at the same DNA and say that while they recognize its intricate complexity and don't have all the answers right now, their research is progressing well in understanding it. They feel they will eventually be able to explain its origin apart from any intelligent cause. Richard Dawkins, one of the world's leading atheists formerly from Oxford, made this very interesting comment:

> "Biology is the study of complicated things that give the appearance of having been designed for a purpose."[28]

Francis Crick, co-discoverer of the DNA molecule structure, made the following statement:

> "Biologists must constantly keep in mind that what they see was not designed, but rather evolved."[29]

The atheist's commitment to denying God's existence limits their interpretation to only naturalistic causes, no matter how unreasonable it might be. They trust that any current significant challenges to their beliefs will be resolved by future research.

Here's where it gets much more interesting. Let's consider a third person, another skeptic ... let's say another atheist. They might look at the same DNA and say something like, "You Christian's are right. There's no way that DNA formed by undirected processes in nature. It was definitely designed. However, it wasn't your God that did it. It was aliens!"

Now, some of you are thinking this last scenario is a bit silly and no serious person would consider it. How about Dr. Francis Crick? He was a highly intelligent scientist; however, he was also an atheist. Initially, he assumed DNA had developed through natural processes here on Earth, but the more he discovered its astonishing complexity, the more he realized how incredibly unlikely that was.

> "An honest man, armed with all the knowledge available to us now, could only state that in some sense, the origin of life appears at the moment to be almost a miracle, so many are the conditions which would have had to have been satisfied to get it going."[30]

He ended up believing that billions of years ago, somewhere else in the universe, aliens created life in seed form and sent it to our planet. These "life seeds" then evolved into every  other life form on the planet, including human beings, including

Dr. Francis Crick himself! This theory is known as "directed panspermia."

Did he believe this seemingly silly idea because he was not smart enough to see its futility? Not at all! He was incredibly intelligent. He didn't need more "facts," he needed a different "starting point" (i.e., worldview) to interpret the facts of which he was already well-aware. We'll be discussing "starting points" again a bit later in this book.

Here we have three different people looking at the exact same evidence (or facts), coming up with three different conclusions. There's obviously got to be more to it than "just the facts." This is where one's worldview comes into play. Your worldview (or starting point) will greatly influence your conclusions and interpretations. Facts alone don't "prove" anything. All facts have to be interpreted, which is much more subjective.

Another way of looking at this is that we've got the order all wrong. Most people think that you (a) look at the evidence, (b) come to some conclusion and then (c) determine which worldview is correct. In reality, it's just the opposite. You (a) start with your worldview, (b) use it to interpret or evaluate the evidence and then (c) come to some conclusion.

As an example of this, consider the following from Stephen Hawking who was considered by most to be the world's leading theoretical physicist:

"However we are not able to make cosmological models without some admixture of ideology."[31]

Hawking was simply saying that you cannot develop a model regarding the origin and operation of the universe in a completely unbiased manner. It's always influenced by your pre-existing ideology (i.e., your worldview or starting point).

2. Arguing from ignorance.

Skeptics have stated, "Just because you don't know how something could have happened on its own, doesn't automatically mean that God supernaturally did it." I would actually agree with this logic. It could very well be that there is a natural explanation that we haven't discovered yet. Some ancient pagans believed that thunder and lightning was a result of the gods being angry. We know better today. Now we realize these things are caused by the gods having a bowling tournament! Ok, maybe not. Seriously though, we know there are perfectly normal natural explanations for these phenomena. Specifically, electrical charges build up within storm clouds causing electrical imbalances between the clouds and the ground. The lightening we see is the discharge which balances everything out again, and the thunderclap is due to the rapid expansion and contraction of the air immediately surrounding the lightning bolt.

Even so, I believe there are many things that truly have no reasonable natural explanation and there's nothing in modern science that would give us reason to believe we will ever discover one. Therefore, the most reasonable and logical deduction is to conclude that what we see is the result of intentional design. The exercise of this "reasonable faith" stands in stark contrast to the skeptic's allegation of Christians embracing "blind faith."

One additional point. When the skeptic engages in this type of a discussion (i.e., natural vs supernatural events), they are guilty of a logical fallacy called bifurcation. This is when someone says it must be one of two options, when in reality there are other possibilities. In this case, they say everything is either natural or supernatural. The specific problem arising in this situation is the skeptic sees supernatural events as being attributed to God and natural events not being attributed to God. There is, however, another (correct) view. All natural events are simply flowing in accordance with the laws God established to guide the day-to-day occurrences within the universe. So even the "natural" events are a result of Divine agency, in that, the laws of science themselves were supernaturally created at the beginning of time. Nature cannot account for its own laws!

3. Anyone Can Be Wrong

It could be that we ourselves will discover some new evidence that indicates we were wrong about our own understanding. Making an erroneous assumption is something that happens to all of us at some point, even though we had been reasonably confident about it for years. It can be a humbling experience, and we are often hesitant to admit our error or misunderstanding. It's part of our fallen human nature for the Christian and the skeptic alike. Many scientists have been wrong about their beliefs. It's quite a rude awakening for them to face the public, having boldly (and sometimes arrogantly) promoted some concept, only to have to admit they were completely wrong.

(See chapter 5 for a few examples of when scientists were wrong.)

4. Inadequacy of Reason or Facts Alone

If someone can logically reason their way into belief in God, then they can logically reason their way out. If looking at the evidence can make someone conclude that God does exist, then theoretically, it should be possible for someone to look at the evidence and conclude that God does NOT exist. When depending solely upon the evidence at hand, others may change their mind back and forth as new evidence is revealed. They may even change their mind simply by reevaluating the existing evidence (i.e., without having any additional facts).

It might also imply that the more evidence you have, the more you would believe in God. Therefore, the *less* intelligent you are, the *less* likely you will believe in God; and conversely, the *more* intelligent you are, the *more* likely you are to believe in God. This flies in the face of reality. There are numerous, extremely intelligent scientists who strongly believe in God, but there are also numerous, extremely intelligent scientists who strongly do not believe in God. So, it can't just be a matter of how many "facts" you have in your head that determines your beliefs about God.

5. Letting the skeptic be the judge.

Where do you most often hear evidence being presented? Typically, in a courtroom situation. The lawyers present their case (including the facts and evidence) to the judge (and sometimes the jury). Then the judge (and/or jury) weighs the facts and evidence on both sides and decides "the truth of the matter."

When you give "evidence" to the skeptic, you
are giving evidence to someone who doesn't
think correctly. Why would I say that? I
am certainly not trying to be disrespectful
or condescending. The reason I draw this
conclusion is because of what we learn from
God's Word.

> because, although they knew God, they did not glorify
> Him as God, nor were thankful, but became futile in their
> thoughts, and their foolish hearts were darkened. Professing
> to be wise, they became fools (Romans 1:21-22).

This is not God engaging in name-calling. He is simply describing
the thinking process of those who have rejected Him. Their thinking
has become "foolish." Therefore, when you give evidence to the
skeptic, most often, they'll disagree with you. We often ask, "How
can they not see this?" Well, this passage in Romans tells us why
"they just don't see it," so we shouldn't be surprised. ***Ultimately,
this is a spiritual issue, not simply an academic debate.*** We need to
understand where they are coming from and not naively think that if
we just give them enough facts, that will change their mind. The facts
may mean little to nothing if there's no spiritual element, specifically
the work of the Holy Spirit. This is not to say that sharing facts is
of no value whatsoever, it just needs to be accompanied by prayer
and a gracious spirit. We'll learn more about sharing these "facts"
a bit later.

6. Elevating the Authority of Science over the Bible

"Science proves the Bible!" I wish I had a nickel for every time I've said that in the past. (I'd have $1.05 by now. OK, probably a lot more!) To most Christians, this phrase sounds great and is certainly perceived as being an encouragement to their faith. However, I've had to recant and refine my apologetic approach, because this is not a biblically proper approach.

When we claim "science proves the Bible," we are inherently saying that science serves as the higher authority which positions science to tell us whether or not the Bible is really true. Do you see the danger in that? Do you see the error in this logic? If science can tell us whether or not the Bible is true, then what do we do if "science" discovers something that doesn't look so good for the Bible? (When I use the term "science," I really mean various conclusions that come out of the scientific community, which in reality are always tentative, subject to future refinement or retraction.) If the scientific community makes a claim that seems directly contradictory to the clear teaching of the Bible, we would have to say, "Well, maybe the Bible is not true, or at least part of it." Perhaps a couple months down the road, "science" discovers something else, which now looks pretty good again for the Bible. Then maybe we would say, "I guess the Bible is true, after all!" Then still later, something else is discovered contrary to God's Word, so once again maybe it isn't true. Now it is true, now it's not, now it is true, now it's not . . . Who would ever be able to trust God's Word? The jury would always be out, because you would never know what's going to happen next.

Elevating science in authority over God's Word means the Bible is then *not* our "ultimate authority." We would constantly have to turn to science to see if what we are reading can be taken seriously or not. You would be bowing to the thoughts and conclusions of men and women who (1) were not there in the beginning, (2) don't know everything, (3) sometimes make mistakes, (4) sometimes even lie and (5) are studying a fallen world which is not the way God made it to begin with. Considering all of this, it is very easy to see why incorrect judgments can be made when they are looking at the world around us and trying to explain its origin.

Just to be clear, I am not saying scientists have no realm of authority. If I want to know which cell phone gets the best reception, or which flat panel TV screen has the highest picture resolution, I feel I can pretty consistently rely on the reports I receive. I won't bother "searching the Scriptures" for those things. However, when it comes to *historical science*, the Bible clearly should be our go-to guide. Science can then help to fill in some details when Scripture leaves those things out. (See chapter 4 for further explanation of *operational* and *historical* science, if you haven't already read that.)

Ultimately, we don't use science to "prove" the Bible; we use the Bible to properly understand science. That statement would understandably make a skeptic's skin crawl, but it's true and it's a very important principle. (To understand this better, see Appendix A)

7. Skeptics Know God Exists

There are no atheists! There never have been and there never will be. You're probably thinking, "Wait a minute ... how in the world can you say that?" You probably even know some atheists. (Maybe you, the reader, are an atheist.) Do I say this because I have read every single philosophy book available and realized all the authors are wrong? No. Is it because I've interviewed all the atheists and determined they are all wrong? No. Then why in the world would I make that extremely strange, and possibly arrogant sounding, claim? It's because I've read God's Word . . .

> because what may be known of God is manifest in them, for God has shown it to them. For since the creation of the world His invisible attributes are clearly seen, being understood by the things that are made, even His eternal power and Godhead, so that they are without excuse (Romans 1:19-20).

The atheist already knows that God exists, because God has clearly made Himself known to them including through nature itself. God demonstrated His existence so much so, that He said they are "without excuse." So, everyone knows that God exists.

Therefore, when we as Christians run around trying to "prove" God's existence, God, in essences, says to us, "What are you doing? They already know I exist." The atheist's claim that they don't know God exists is not due to a simple lack of knowledge that a quick infusion of brilliance from an occasionally over-zealous Christian can fix. This is ultimately a spiritual issue and a decision of their will to reject God.

Now, there are those who have chosen to reject all the evidence and the direct knowledge from God, and they call themselves "atheists." They are not people who don't know God exists; they're just people who have consciously chosen to reject the evidence and deny Him. God is not going to force them to believe in Him, so He says, "OK, I'm not going to force your hand here, but there are consequences for rejecting me." He then goes on in the remainder of Romans 1 to describe what those consequences are.

> because, although they knew God, they did not glorify Him as God, nor were thankful, but became futile in their thoughts, and their foolish hearts were darkened. Professing to be wise, they became fools, and changed the glory of the incorruptible God into an image made like corruptible man—and birds and four-footed animals and creeping things.

> Therefore God also gave them up to uncleanness, in the lusts of their hearts, to dishonor their bodies among themselves, who exchanged the truth of God for the lie, and worshiped and served the creature rather than the Creator, who is blessed forever. Amen.

> For this reason God gave them up to vile passions. For even their women exchanged the natural use for what is against nature. Likewise also the men, leaving the natural use of the woman, burned in their lust for one another, men with men committing what is shameful, and receiving in themselves the penalty of their error which was due.

> And even as they did not like to retain God in their knowledge, God gave them over to a debased mind, to do those things which are not fitting; being filled with all unrighteousness, sexual immorality, wickedness, covetousness, maliciousness; full of envy, murder, strife, deceit, evil-mindedness; they are whisperers, backbiters, haters of God, violent, proud, boasters, inventors of evil things, disobedient to parents, undiscerning, untrustworthy, unloving, unforgiving,

unmerciful; who, knowing the righteous judgment of God, that those who practice such things are deserving of death, not only do the same but also approve of those who practice them (Romans 1:21-32).

So, what I meant when I said, "There are no atheists," is there aren't any people who don't know God exists, only those who have chosen to reject that knowledge. These skeptics call themselves atheists and subsequently experience the consequences of doing so, which includes not being able to think clearly regarding spiritual matters.

So there have always been atheists and there always will be. And now you know what I mean by that!

Because of these seven reasons, we should not use evidence in an attempt to prove our beliefs.

So What Good is Evidence?

Many of you have probably studied a lot of evidence for the validity of the Christian worldview and are frustrated now, thinking I am telling you evidence is of no value. On the contrary, not only is evidence extremely valuable, but it is biblically necessary in order to avoid having a blind faith based on nothing more than "wishful thinking." We just do not use the evidence as "proof" and we don't need to either. We use evidence in a slightly different manner which we will discuss in the next chapter.

In chapter 9, we will use worldviews to evaluate evidence and will clearly see how the Christian worldview is the only one that makes sense of all that we see around us (i.e., the evidence). We will also see how the skeptic's worldview struggles to make sense of the world all along the way and often proves itself self-contradictory.

9

Philosophy Through the Prism of Worldviews

We've spent some time up to this point explaining the approach to proving God's existence, as well as the nature of evidence itself. As mentioned at the close of the last chapter, this sometimes leads to the impression that evidence of is no use and somehow it is wrong to rely on it when witnessing. This, however, is a mistaken conclusion. We read in 1 Peter 3:15 that we are to "be ready to give a defense to everyone who asks you a reason for the hope that is in you, with meekness and fear." This requires having evidence for what we claim to believe.

On numerous occasions, I have been approached by individuals after one of my presentations, telling me something like, "That was great, but I don't need to know any of that. I just believe." They are always very sincere and well-intended in sharing that with me, but there's a problem with their logic. They essentially are stating that their faith is so strong, they don't need reasons. They already believe, so why worry about understanding all these apologetic arguments, especially when it does take a fair amount of effort. The problem is this . . . if they don't really have tangible reasons as to why they believe what they do, why should anyone else believe it? How do they know it's true themselves, other than just believing they are right? How in the world do they mentor their own children? Why should their children believe it when they as the parents can't really defend why it is true? How is their faith any different than a Mormon's faith or anyone else's? If they do witness to someone, they essentially would be telling that person to "trust them," that they have somehow figured out the truth, even though they can't explain how they know it's true. This logic really places the focus on us, and we certainly don't want that!

Ultimately, we don't want people to "trust us," we want them to trust God and His Word. However, if we can't give them any reason to consider it, other than that's what we believe, what motivation do they have to listen to us or choose the Bible over Hinduism, Buddhism, atheism or any other worldview?

Consider this passage from the book of Jude:

> "Beloved, while I was very diligent to write to you (A) concerning our common salvation, I found it necessary to write to you exhorting (B)you to contend earnestly for the faith which was once for all delivered to the saints" (Jude 1:3).

Earnestly contending for the faith requires us to have reasons which are biblically, logically and scientifically sound. (In reality, if our reasons are biblically sound, they will automatically be logically and scientifically sound.)

Philosophy Through the Prism of Worldviews

It is not my intention to write a treatise on all worldviews in this particular book, but primarily to contrast the biblical worldview against a general skeptic's or atheist's worldview. The main principles I share will often apply across all worldviews.

Our ultimate goal is to help the skeptic realize that if they don't adopt the Christian worldview as their starting point, they don't have a rational basis for trying to make sense of anything at all. Sounds like a bold claim, but it's true and will be evident to you as you continue reading. If you can help the skeptic understand the inherent weaknesses in their own worldview, they will be able to "connect the dots" on their own. They will usually realize that if their "starting point" is faulty, using it to answer life's most critical questions will inevitably lead to erroneous conclusions.

Philosophy & Science

We are going to evaluate both philosophy and science through the prism of worldviews. That is, we are going to attempt to philosophically and scientifically address some very critical questions given each of the two juxtaposed worldviews. Which worldview is consistently capable of yielding sensible, logically consistent answers, without having to contort itself or flat-out contradict itself along the way?

In each case, we will use hypothetical conversations to see how each worldview deals with the topic at hand.

Philosophical Test #1: Logic

Our first philosophical concept focuses on *logic*. Specifically, how does each worldview account for the existence of logic?

Atheistic Worldview

You can ask the skeptic (for now, let's say an atheist), "Do you believe that logic exists?" They will most likely look at you very strangely and may be somewhat annoyed, perceiving that this is a silly question. They may respond by saying, "Of course I believe in logic! Why would you even ask that?" You can then proceed with the following conversation, in which you will see my suggestions as to what to ask, as well as what their response will most likely be.

Christian: "Do you believe there are laws of logic, such as the Law of Non-Contradiction? For example, I cannot be both standing here talking to you and NOT standing here talking to you."

Atheist: "Yes, I believe there are laws of logic."

Christian: "Do you believe these laws are physical things? Can I take them into a laboratory and weigh them? Can I paint them and bend them in half, etc.?"

Atheist: "No, they're not physical things, they are non-physical or abstract."

Christian: "Do you believe the laws of logic are the same everywhere? Are they the same here as they are in Pocatello, Idaho, and are the same on the moon, or are they different in different places?"

Atheist: "They're the same everywhere!"

Christian: "Do these laws stay the same? Are they the same today as they were yesterday? Will they be the same next year as they are today or do they change?"

Atheist: "No, they don't change . . . they stay the same."

Christian: "Alright, so you believe there are laws of logic that are non-physical, universal (the same everywhere), and they are unchanging."

Atheist: "Yes, that's what I believe."

Christian: "OK. Then I have one additional question for you . . . Where did these laws come from? Using your worldview (the one you've chosen by your own free will), tell me where these laws of logic came from. I'm confused, because being an atheist, you believe the only thing that exists is physical stuff . . . matter and energy, but scientists don't believe that matter and energy can create non-physical things. Yet you believe that the laws of logic are non-physical. Using your worldview, please explain to me how you know they are the same everywhere. What in your worldview tells you that they must be the same everywhere? Finally, tell me how you know they do not change. What in your worldview dictates that they cannot change?"

In reality, there is nothing in the atheist's worldview that can account for the existence of logic. And it certainly cannot explain why the laws of logic should be universally the same and never change. Yes, the atheist truly does believe in logic, uses it (albeit not always very consistently), and expects you to be logical as well. However, their own worldview cannot even account for the existence of logic.

So, did we just disprove the atheistic worldview? Yes, we did! There is no rational rebuttal to this point. And think about this, if you can't account for the laws of logic, you're done! Why? Because you need logic to discuss anything else! This argument in and of itself refutes atheism and constitutes a form of proof for theism.

We've just concluded that the atheistic worldview has a huge struggle when it comes to explaining the existence of logic, but how does the Christian worldview account for it? Let's take a look.

Christian Worldview

Christians believe (as their part of their starting point) that God exists and that He is . . . non-physical, universal, and unchanging! Furthermore, we believe that God created a world that operates under the laws of logic which themselves are . . . non-physical, universal, and unchanging. They reflect His character and are hallmarks of His creation! The existence of logic makes perfect sense in a Christian worldview, but it is completely antithetical to the atheistic worldview. If you think about this further, an atheist would have to assume that the Christian worldview is correct, in order to justify belief in the laws of logic and then turn around and use those laws to tell you that God doesn't exist. Pardon the pun, but at this point, we are just being . . . logical.

On a similar note, you could also consider where the laws of science came from? The skeptic certainly believes in "laws of science," so it is only natural to ask how his or her worldview explains their origins. We  are not focusing on the simple formulation of these laws which entails a point in time where scientists recognized regularities in nature and decided to officially document them in written form. We are focusing more so on how these laws (i.e., phenomenological principles) came about to begin with.

Thinking this through, you can ask which came first . . . matter and energy or the laws that guide and restrict their interactions? Is it the case that matter and energy somehow popped into existence, but sat around thinking, "We'd love to do something here, but there are no laws to tell us what we can and cannot do." Or maybe the laws magically appeared out of nowhere, saying something like, "We've got all these great ideas and parameters that will be very useful. Now . . . if we just had something to which we could apply them. Oh well, maybe someday." It's beyond a stretch of the imagination to envision how "laws of science" somehow came into existence from nowhere for no reason. It's completely unreasonable and illogical to think that they created themselves, and there's nothing in our own experience that indicates that matter and energy could have produced something immaterial such as the laws of science. How would matter and energy do anything before there were laws to guide and restrict them? To believe they both (matter/energy and the laws of science) sprang into existence at the same time completely independent of any outside intervention is an even bigger stretch of the imagination, requiring an unbelievable amount of "faith" in the "almighty power of nothing." For the atheist, it seems miracles are allowed in science as long as "nothing" produces them, rather than "something" or someone.

On the other hand, the existence of the laws of science makes perfect sense in the Christian worldview. God is a god of order (1 Corinthians 14:33), and we would expect there to be order and regularity in His creation. You may remember reading in chapter 4 that most major areas of science were founded by Bible-believing Christians. Here's an additional quote documenting this fact:

> "Strange as it may seem, the Bible played a positive role in the development of science. ... Had it not been for the rise of the literal interpretation of the Bible and the subsequent appropriation of biblical narratives by early modern scientists, modern science may not have arisen at all. In sum,

the Bible and its literal interpretation have played a vital role in the development of Western science."[32]

Here's one more quote emphasizing that the emergence of science as a practice wasn't due to a general belief in some generic supernatural power who is now uninterested in our lives (i.e., *deism*), but a more personal God (such as in the Christian worldview):

> "Science was not the work of western secularists or even deists; it was entirely the work of devout believers in an active, conscious, creator God."[33]

Anyone who claims that no real scientist believes the Bible, not only does not understand *science* very well, they don't know history either. Science was berthed out of the Christian worldview.

Philosophical Test #2: Absolute Morality

Our second philosophical example has to do with *absolute morality*. Before we delve into comparing worldviews, I need to explain what I mean by absolute morality. Is it acceptable to  listen to loud music? A very natural question arises when trying to espouse an answer: What do you consider loud? It's a subjective assessment. What might be loud to one person, might not be loud at all to another. Even if we could agree on what defines "loud," we might still be at odds as to whether or not it is acceptable. Furthermore, it may be acceptable in some circumstances and not others. Volume is all very relative.

When considering the topic of morality, we certainly could be talking about something that is very subjective. However, certain things seem to be very apparent to the vast majority of people. For instance, most well-adjusted people would say that it is wrong to torture your pets for no particular reason. It doesn't matter what day of the week it is or whether you live in Maine or Zimbabwe or whether or not it is raining. Torturing pets is just wrong. The same would go for murdering someone because you don't like the color of their hat. Again, we seem to intrinsically know murder would be wrong. Torturing pets and murdering people are not *relative* issues to most people. Rather, they are *absolute* issues. This is where the idea of "absolute morality" comes into play in our Philosophical Tests. Let's focus on absolute morality vs relative morality as we continue testing our two worldviews.

Atheistic Worldview

Within the atheistic worldview, why is it that people all over the world tend to intrinsically sense or know that murder is wrong? Yes, there are always exceptions where certain individuals experience cognitive anomalies, and they seem not to have a normal sense of right and wrong. But we are talking about accounting for the fact that the vast majority of people all around the world agree that murder is wrong, even without specifically having been taught this.

The response to this question might look something like the following conversation:

Atheist: "It has to do with how we've evolved over millions of years."

Christian: "Evolution? That's the natural selection and survival-of-the-fittest, right?"

Atheist: "Yes."

Christian: "So, if Christians feel they are being threatened by atheists and maybe are more fit or outnumber them, we can just decide to exterminate atheists from the planet. It won't truly be wrong for us to do this because we would just be using our instincts to survive in whatever way works best for us. That's how evolution works, isn't it? In fact, you believe we owe our existence to this process operating over millions and millions of years, correct?"

Atheist: "Well, no, you can't do that. That's murder!"

Christian: "I agree that it would be murder, but why would it be wrong?"

Atheist: "There are laws against that!"

Christian: "I know there are laws against it, but why would it be wrong in and of itself? Why do we make laws against this?"

Atheist: "Because it helps society?"

Christian: "Why should I care about society? Why can't I just look out for myself?"

Atheist: "We need society to work together for the benefit of everyone as a whole!"

Christian: "Why should I care about everyone as a whole? If it's survival of the fittest, if I am more fit, why can't I just do what I want? Why should I have to conform to what someone else tells me is good for society? If others can't make it on their own, maybe they should be eliminated."

Atheist: "That's crazy! You shouldn't just think of yourself!"

Christian: "I actually agree with you, but I am wondering what in your worldview justifies why you should care about others? In fact, how can you use the word 'should' in any of your arguments? That implies an overarching, unified moral code against which you judge everything. Your worldview, however, does not support the existence of such an *absolute moral* law."

Atheist: "Well, it's not so much that it's ultimately wrong; it's the way we evolved . . . the way chemicals react in your brain. That gives you the impression or sensation that murder is wrong and it's a useful thing to further our species."

Christian: "Oh, so morality evolved by accident and is ultimately the result of chemicals flowing in our brains."

Atheist: "Yes."

Christian: "So, if the chemicals in my brain happen to flow differently than yours, I can do whatever they are leading me to do, including eliminating you, and no one can really say I was wrong for doing so. In fact, when Hitler was instrumental in the genocide of millions of Jews and other groups of people, he was just 'helping evolution along' and you can't say that what he did was truly wrong. You might not like what he did. You might feel it was not helpful, but you can't actually say it was absolutely wrong."

Atheist: "I think what Hitler did was evil!"

Christian: "Evil? How do you define 'evil'? In order for there to be 'evil' there has to be something that is 'good.' But for anything to be truly good or evil, there must be *a standard* against which everything is measured. The problem, once again, is that your worldview is incapable of supporting such a standard. Everything is truly relative. What might seem evil to you, might seem good to me and vice versa. You may think that when people raise their children to believe in God and the Bible, that's evil, but you have no absolute basis for making such a claim. Those would just be your thoughts and they should carry no more weight than anyone else's."

This type of conversation can go on and on, but I think you get the gist of the argument.

Here's an interesting quote from atheist James Robert Brown:

> You can't just make up facts, including moral facts; you're
> under obligation, moral obligation without God, you don't
> need God for this, you have a moral obligation to not murder,
> not rob people … All I ask you to do is believe there's no
> God but still murder is wrong. There are moral facts, as well
> as physical facts, as well as mathematical facts, that's all I'm
> asking … It's just a basic fact, a basic moral fact, that murder
> is wrong.[34]

Brown (the atheist) claimed there are "moral facts." Just where did
these moral facts come from? Did they evolve over time? They must
have, because according to him all life came through the process of
Darwinian evolution. How do we go about determining what they
are? What do we do when different people have varying opinions
as to what they are and who they apply to? This is a complete can
of worms, but it's the kind of response you get when you attempt to
account for these intrinsic moral laws without referring to a moral
law giver!

To illustrate this further, here's a conversation I had with a co-worker
(at a secular company, years ago). We were the only ones in the office
at the time and he said something that I just couldn't let go. He and
I had a good relationship, so I knew he wouldn't mind me pushing
him a bit on this. We'll jump into the middle of the conversation.

Co-worker: "Yeah, I guess that's because I'm a good person."

Me: "You feel you're a good person?"

Co-worker: "Sure!"

Me: "How do you define *good*?"

Co-worker: "Well, you know, *moral.*"

Me: "How do you define *moral*?"

Co-worker: Bit of a pause. "Um ... Well ... Majority opinion."

Me: "Majority opinion?"

Co-worker: "Yes."

Me: "So, what Hitler did in exterminating millions of Jews and people from other ethnic groups, that was alright, because the majority of Hitler's followers were supportive of his leadership?"

Co-worker: "Well, no. That was wrong."

Me: "But you said *majority opinion.*"

Co-worker: "Well, not for that."

Me: "So just how do you determine *majority opinion*? By vote? Is it a country-by-country thing? Is it state-by-state? Maybe county-by-county? What do you do when you cross the state or county line? Do you have to be aware of details of each sector's moral law? And even if it is state-by-state, how often do you vote to see if the majority opinion has changed? Do you vote once every 5 years? Once every year?"

Co-worker: "Oh, I don't know. Just forget it altogether!"

We both laughed a bit because he realized that I was purposely giving him a hard time. However, I was simply asking follow-up questions to a bold claim he made. In doing so, he clearly saw there was no basis for the validity of that claim.

Here's another frightening citation from Communist leader Mao Zedong, Founder of the People's Republic of China:

> "I do not agree with the view that to be moral, the motive of one's action has to be benefiting others. Morality does not have to be defined in relation to others… People like me want to… satisfy our hearts to the full, and in doing so we automatically have the most valuable moral codes. Of course there are people and objects in the world, but they are all there only for me… People like me only have a duty to ourselves; we have no duty to other people… Some say one has a responsibility for history. I don't believe it. I am only concerned about developing myself."[35]

Did that type of a mindset possibly lead to anything bad? Take a look at this excerpt from the Washington Post:

> Who was the biggest mass murderer in the history of

the world? Most people probably assume that the answer is Adolf Hitler, architect of the Holocaust. Others might guess Soviet dictator Joseph Stalin, who may indeed have managed to kill even more innocent people than Hitler did, many of them as part of a terror famine that likely took more lives than the Holocaust. But both Hitler and Stalin were outdone by Mao Zedong. From 1958 to 1962, his Great Leap Forward policy led to the deaths of up to 45 million people – easily making it the biggest episode of mass murder ever recorded.[36]

Unbelievably tragic! I am certainly not saying atheism leads to becoming a murderer. What I am saying is there is nothing within the atheistic worldview that can serve as a basis for condemning murder. Why are most atheists not murders? Even though most atheists would deny it, I believe it's because they were created in the image of God and thus were instilled with the moral knowledge of good and evil. Therefore, atheists have a moral conscience and generally live by those inherent principles, even while denying moral absolutes came from their Creator.

Christian Worldview

Turning the tables once again, how does the Christian deal with the idea of murder being wrong or the idea of absolute morality in general? Very simply. God created this universe and everything in it. He owns it. It's His and He has the right to "set the rules." He specifically gave us Ten Commandments, the sixth of which states, "You shall not murder" (Exodus 20:13). In the Christian worldview, murder is not deemed wrong because it is harmful to society; **it is wrong because it violates God's Holy standard**, which is the ultimate, universal standard for all of humanity. This explains why it is *wrong*, but the reason we intrinsically *know* it's wrong is that we are created in the image of God and He has placed this knowledge within us.

> Which shew the work of the law written in their hearts, their conscience also bearing witness, and their thoughts the mean while accusing or else excusing one another (Romans 2:15).

In summary, while the atheistic worldview has no basis for explaining why most people universally believe in moral absolutes, the Christian worldview can account for this in a straightforward, coherent way that is completely consistent with our belief system.

Philosophical Test #3: Knowledge & Certainty

Our third and final philosophical test has to do with knowledge or the ability to actually know things. You have to hang in there a bit for this one. It might seem like it's getting "weird," but let's think through this logically. There is a very important point in all of this, otherwise I wouldn't be taking the time to develop this example.

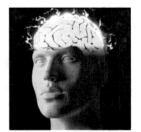

Atheistic Worldview

You could have the following conversation with the skeptic/atheist:

Christian: "Is there anything you know for certain? Anything you know absolutely for sure?"

Atheist: "Well, I guess I know I am here right now."

Christian: "How do you know you're here?"

Atheist: "Because I'm talking to you."

Christian: "How do you know you are not just dreaming that you are talking to me?"

Atheist: "Because you are responding back?"

Christian: "How do you know you are not just dreaming that I am responding back?"

Atheist: "Well, because I can pinch myself and I can feel it."

Christian: "How do you know you are not just dreaming that you pinched yourself and could feel it?"

Atheist: "Well, I just somehow know that I am really here."

At this point, the atheist might concede that they don't really know for sure they are actually there, but then I explain that even though they don't know for sure, there is certainly enough evidence to accept their existence as a *virtual* certainty. Ultimately, however, they can't say they know for sure.

Here's another angle on this before we get to the main point. Let's say

I told you that my next door neighbor's oldest son was 27 years old, but I could be wrong. Do I really know he's 27 if I am telling you that there's a chance I could be wrong? No, I don't know for sure. I may feel fairly confident, but I can't really be absolutely certain, if I'm admitting I could be wrong. Alright, with this simple analogy, let's proceed with our main point. (It gets better!)

The following conversation demonstrates how we test our worldviews in the area of knowledge and certainty:

Christian: "Out of all of the knowledge that is possible in the universe, what percentage do you think you possess?"

Atheist: "Wow, that's kind of a hard question to answer. I'm not sure what the percentage would be, but I guess it would be pretty small."

Christian: "I know what you mean, and I would say mine would also be very, very small. For argument sake, however, let's say you thought you knew 1% of everything there is to know. Now that's probably a lot more than either of us really know, but let's humor ourselves. Is it at all possible that something out there in the 99% you admit you don't know would reveal that you were actually wrong about something you thought you knew within the 1%? Is that at least possible?"

Atheist: "Yeah, I guess."

Christian: "So, if it's possible something in the unknown 99% would show you were wrong about the 1%, then you don't really even know the 1% for sure either. In fact, it's actually possible you could be wrong about everything you think you know, which means you can't know anything for sure."

Atheist: "Yeah, well you can't either."

Christian: "Are you sure about that? Actually, you can't even know that I can't know anything."

Atheist: "This is getting crazy and juvenile."

Christian: "I admit that in a sense this sounds kind of juvenile. However, I am simply pointing out the fact that given your chosen worldview, you have no real basis for claiming to know anything for sure."

Atheist: "Well, I don't know how your situation would be any different than mine."

Is the atheist right? Are we no better off? You might not know how to respond to this claim so let's take a minute to examine whether or not the Christian worldview fairs any better than the atheist's in this regard.

Christian Worldview

There is one way you could know something for sure… if you actually knew everything! That way there's no chance of ever discovering something new that exposes the fact you were wrong about what you thought you knew. Well, if you're like me, you realize very quickly that this isn't a realistic option. Nobody knows everything, not even close.

However, there is actually one other way you could know something for sure. What if you knew someone who knew everything, and that "person" decided to tell you something in a way you could understand, and they did not lie? That's the Christian worldview! We believe in God, who knows everything, and He chose to tell us certain things and He does not lie! A Christian actually has a philosophical basis (within their own worldview) for claiming to know something for sure, whereas an atheist has to admit they could be wrong about everything!

Should we use this argument to tell the atheist that we are right about everything we believe? No. We are simply pointing out that while his or her worldview does not support the idea of truly being able to have certainty about anything they believe, the Christian's worldview has a solid basis for claiming to know something for sure. We are simply testing worldviews, and once again, the Christian worldview handles the topic very naturally and consistently, while the atheist's worldview struggles to account for it at all.

Reminder: As you discuss these types of issues, be very careful not to be condescending, judgmental or arrogant. Your goal is to help them see the shortcomings in their own worldview and realize that if their starting point is faulty, the conclusions drawn from it will likely be faulty as well. Your caring demeanor will be especially necessary for them to be willing to stick with you because, at least internally, they will most likely be reeling from the "attack" on their core being. No one naturally responds well to such a situation, not even Christians.

So, let's be particularly gracious and make sure they know we are there because we truly care about them and are not just interested in winning an argument by using some cleaver lines of reasoning.

Having examined our two worldviews philosophically, in the next chapter we will continue our examination by conducting some scientific tests. I think you'll enjoy it!

10

Science through the
Prism of Worldviews

We've just finished discussing philosophy through a filter of worldviews. Next, we'll switch gears and use the same filters to take a look at the nature of science itself.

Science Through the Prism of Worldviews

We are now going to see how each of the two major worldviews

accounts for the existence and nature of science itself. That is, which of the two worldviews intrinsically serves as a better basis for the concept of science and, as well as attempts made within science to 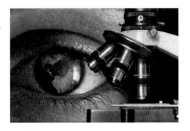 explain various physical phenomenon of the world in which we live.

We'll take a look a just three scientifically related examples.

Since each of these situations involves events that happened in the distant past when no one was around to observe them, they fall into the category of what we call "historical science." These events were not observed, cannot be repeated, and cannot be directly tested by science. It is very similar to what occurs at a crime scene investigation where there were no witnesses. There are three major distinctions related to this type of a situation. (1) The event was not observed as it occurred by any of those involved in the investigation. (2) The event itself cannot be repeated because it was a one-time incident and we cannot have the exact same people and objects play it out exactly as it originally happened, with the same circumstances at the exact same point in time. Not only has that time already passed, with all of its numerous specific characteristics, but we don't even know what all of those factors were. (3) The situation cannot be tested directly because it was in the past and is not now occurring in the same way for us to directly examine. What we can do is make observations of what we do see in the present and formulate educated guesses as to what most likely occurred in the past. For more information on this, see chapter 4 regarding how science works in general.

Because worldviews involve opinions as to what has occurred in the past, predictions can be made as to what we would expect to observe in the present related to each of these views. As we examine these worldviews, we will be taking a look at what each would predict (regarding whatever is scientifically being considered within that test) and comparing these predictions to what we actually observe to be true today.

Scientific Example #1: The Origin of the Universe

Our first example deals with the origin of the physical universe as a whole. (We'll save commenting on the variety of life for the second example.) Let's look at what each worldview posits about this event.

Atheistic Worldview

The atheist worldview asserts that the universe came into existence on its own, without any purpose or outside intervention. Atheists look only to the physical laws of nature to explain this event. The "Big Bang" is currently the most widely accepted model related to the origin of the universe.

Christian Worldview

The Christian worldview espouses that God supernaturally called the universe into existence out of nothing (Genesis 1:1, John 1:3, Psalm 33:6).

What does the evidence indicate?

I've written extensively about what the evidence indicates in my first book, *Creation & Evolution: Compatible or In Conflict*, as well as addressing it in various videos and articles. We cannot do it justice here, but my intention within the context of this book is to simply highlight a few pertinent issues. The two relevant concepts we'll briefly cover are (a) the laws of thermodynamics and (b) something called the "anthropic principle."

Laws of Thermodynamics

Thermodynamics is the study of the relationship between heat, work, temperature, and energy. There are four main laws of thermodynamics (the zeroth through the third). For our discussion, we will be looking at the first and second. In a simplistic sense, the first law relates to "quantity" and the second relates to "quality."

The First Law conveys the idea that matter can neither be created from nothing, nor completely destroyed. The Second Law states that the amount of useable energy in a given system always trends downward, meaning that over time, there is less and less available energy for work. These constitute arguably the best "proven" laws in science. Any theory that violates one of these laws is immediately considered extremely suspect and generally thrown out or significantly modified to comport.

The First Law of Thermodynamics

If the universe came into existence on its own, where did all the energy come from? Just so you understand, the Big Bang is not a "force of nature." It doesn't even explain the true origin of the universe because it doesn't get started until after you have all the energy that now exists. It is simply an attempt at explaining what happened to all that initial energy to convert it into an entire universe. It comes "late to the dance" and then can only somewhat account for the creation of hydrogen, helium and maybe a little bit of lithium (the three lightest gases). It can't even account for the formation of stars galaxies and planets!

So again, where did the literally astronomical amount of energy come from? If you're an atheist, you cannot appeal to the supernatural or even anything physical. Why not something else physical? Because the universe represents all that physically exists, and that's what we're trying to explain! But if the ultimate source is not supernatural and not physical, the only other option left is . . . nothing! The universe ultimately came from nothing! Yes, that's the ruling paradigm. This is where the elite must do a lot of hand waving, misdirecting, and reminding us that they are PhD scientists and we just need to trust them. The atheists sometimes mock the Creationists' Worldview: "Silly people, trying to understand how nothing could produce everything. That's so cute. Don't worry, we've got it all figured out. You'll just have to trust us because it's beyond your comprehension."

But the idea of something coming out of nothing directly violates the First Law of Thermodynamics. So, holding on to this idea leads to a lot of very strange statements and claims. Consider the following:

> Lawrence Krauss (theoretical physicist and Director of the Origins Institute at Arizona State University)

> "Even if you accept this argument that nothing is not nothing, you have to acknowledge that nothing is being used in a philosophical sense. But I don't really give [care] about what 'nothing' means to philosophers; I care about the 'nothing' of reality. And if the 'nothing' of reality is full of stuff, then I'll go with that."[37]

> "The point is it would be amazing to have nothing. There's always going to be something. It's going to arise sometime, somewhere and you happen to live where it is."[38]

Say what? How do these quotes show intellectual superiority?

I want to share one other quote that I always found fascinating. Unfortunately, I don't remember the source because it was from an audio lecture years ago and I didn't think to document it at the time. It was from a scientist; a physicist, if I remember correctly:

> "You have to remember that there's a difference between nothing and absolute nothing!"

The point was that if there truly was "absolute nothing" in the beginning, nothing could ever come from that, but if there was simply "nothing," then you might get a universe out of it! The same scientist made this statement as well:

Picture of Nothing (Photo Credit: nobody!)

> "Even where there's nothing, there's always something going on!"

Can you show me any experiments to verify that? Hello? Hello? Oh, I guess he must have left for the day.

Lawrence Krauss also said;

> "The laws of physics as we understand them make it eminently plausible that our universe arose from nothing — no space, no time, no particles, nothing that we now know of."[39]

Question: Where did the laws of physics come from? And "where" and "when" were they, since time and space didn't exist yet? Apparently, they initially came from nothing and then they allowed matter and energy to come from nothing. What allowed the laws of physics to come from nothing? It's beyond the stretch of any imagination as to how laws of physics could create themselves for no reason and for no pre-planned purpose. Well, maybe not beyond the imagination of some secular scientists. Perhaps they've been reading a bit too much of Lewis Caroll's "Through the Looking-Glass." The following is a short conversation between Alice and the Queen:

> Alice laughed: "There's no use trying," she said. "One can't believe impossible things."
>
> "I daresay you haven't had much practice," said the Queen. "When I was younger, I always did it for half an hour a day. Why, sometimes I've believed as many as six impossible things before breakfast."

Einstein is quoted as saying, "Once you can accept the universe as matter expanding into nothing that is something, wearing stripes with plaid comes easy."[40] Gotta love that one!

I could list many more quotes from scientists that would make your head spin, and many are quite entertaining, as well.

I think it would be wise at this point to turn to the web to get some more sensible information. However, I am not referring to the world wide web (i.e., the internet). I'm talking about *Charlotte's Web*! In one portion of this classic story by E.B. White, the lamb told Wilbur (the pig), "Pigs mean less than nothing to me."

The following is Wilbur's response:

> "What do you mean, less than nothing?" replied Wilbur. "I don't think there is any such thing as less than nothing. Nothing is absolutely the limit of nothingness. It's the lowest you can go. It's the end of the line. How can something be less than nothing? If there were something that was less than nothing, then nothing would not be nothing, it would be something even though it's just a very little bit of something. But if nothing is nothing, then nothing has nothing that is less than it is."[41]

I believe there's more wisdom in this simple children's story than in the gray matter of many highly intelligent scientists. Psalm 111:10 says, "The fear of the Lord is the beginning of wisdom." Many of the elite scientists do not fear (i.e., have a reverent respect for) God. Many do not even believe in God, so it's easy to see how, while being very intelligent, they lack true wisdom (i.e., how to properly apply knowledge). Within the group who do claim to believe in God, many make the mistake of using their own faulty reasoning to decide who and what God is, rather than gleaning those details from God's own revelation in Scripture.

> Trust in the Lord with all your heart, And lean not on your own understanding; In all your ways acknowledge Him, And He shall direct your paths" (Proverbs 3:5-6).

I jokingly say, "Sometimes I impress myself and other times I put the milk back in the dishwasher!" Having a certain level of intelligence is not a guarantee that all your actions and decisions are wise. It has been said that, "Wisdom comes with age," but it's not a requirement! You can just get older without getting wiser. Something for all of us to think about!

Again, I could write an entire book on the origin of the universe. We're just scratching the surface here.

The Second Law of Thermodynamics

Recognizing the problem of trying to get something from nothing, some have resorted to believing the universe is eternal. It had no beginning. You see, no beginning means no need for a "beginner." No "beginner" means no need for God. It's as simple as that. Or is it?

This is where the Second Law of Thermodynamics comes into play. This is also known as the Law of Entropy. Entropy is a measure of the amount of energy in a system which is unavailable to do work. Simply put, the Second Law of Thermodynamics states that for any given system, as energy is transferred or transformed, the amount of energy unavailable to do work always increases. Following this to its logical conclusion, if enough times transpires, all of the energy within the system will be unusable.

So how does this work its way into our discussion on the origin of the universe? If the universe was truly infinitely old (i.e., it had no beginning), all of its energy would have been "used up," so-to-speak. There would be no usable energy left by now. In other words, it would have run out of gas a long time ago. However, we know for a fact, there is a lot of usable or available energy in the universe. Consider our own sun, 93 million miles away. Each hour it produces enough energy to power a light bulb for every person on the entire planet every day for their entire life! And that's just one average sized star. Never mind the estimated 10 trillion trillion stars in the entire universe.

The logical conclusion is that since there's still a significant amount of usable energy in the universe, it cannot be infinitely old! It must have had a beginning. We can then draw attention to the Cosmological Argument, which is as follows:

A.   Anything that begins to exist has a cause.
B.   The universe began to exist.
C.   Therefore, the universe has a cause.

The Second Law of Thermodynamics supports a created beginning of the universe and prohibits its eternality.

The Anthropic Principle

Next, we'll turn our attention to the second element I mentioned we would use for our first scientific test, the Anthropic Principle. This concept addresses the fact that the universe, in some sense, appears to be designed with us in mind. "Anthropos" is Greek for "human." There are numerous factors in nature and in the universe that are "finely tuned." This means that if the current values of these factors were slightly different, life would not be possible. If there were only one or two, you could easily envision them being correct completely by chance. What if there were 12? Twelve components being completely correct might be a bit harder to claim was by random chance. As you increase the number of factors, you get to a point where you would have to say, "Ok, something's going on here. This is starting to look like someone planned this!"

As an overly simplified analogy, let's say you went over to a friend's house to attend a PowerPoint presentation on financial planning. You arrive and find a seat in the living room. There are several "factors" that contribute to a successful presentation. Some of these factors include:

- A screen set up in front of the fireplace.
- A projector sitting on a table in the middle of the living room.
- The presenter's laptop connected to the projector.

If any of these elements are missing or fail to work properly, the presentation cannot proceed successfully as needed. There are even many "sub-factors" involved in this scenario, so let's look at just a few of these critical factors and sub-factors that are necessary for a successful presentation.

- Not just a laptop, but a functioning one, obviously
- A Microsoft-compatible operating system loaded on the laptop
- Microsoft PowerPoint software installed on the laptop
- The pre-designed PowerPoint presentation file
- A remote to control the slides from the front of the living room
- Charged batteries in the remote
- Power for the laptop, either directly plugged in to an outlet or charged batteries
- Power for the projector, meaning it is plugged into an electrical outlet
- A power sub-station which directs the electrical power from

the main power utility plant to the residential home
- An electrical power plant generating electricity
- Employees at the power plant keeping it running

I could list other factors, but this will suffice to make the point that if any one of these is removed, the planned presentation cannot proceed. Yes, the presenter could "wing it" and just try his or her best to explain everything apart from using the intended visuals, but the originally planned presentation is impossible.

That's pretty clear. But here's another point, perhaps more pertinent to our discussion. No one attending that presentation would, for even one second, believe that all those things (the screen, laptop, projector, remote, power sources, etc.) just happened to come together fortuitously, with no outside intentional intervention. It is more than obvious someone (or multiple people) purposely set all of those things up in order to achieve a specified goal, the financial planning presentation.

One additional analogy may be helpful when thinking about the "fine-tuning" aspect of the anthropic principle.

Let's say you are an audio recording engineer. Before you leave the studio each day, you always move the Master Volume control down to 0. Your next project requires that control to be set right at 7. You arrive the next day and find its already positioned right at 7! You ask one of your assistants what happened. They say, "Sorry, my 4-year old son was messing around with the board and he must have set it that way." Would you believe your assistant? Well, there's really no reason not to. It's certainly a plausible story. If the volume scale goes from 0 to 10, and the control was moved randomly, there would be 1 chance in 11 that it would be right where you need it. (Yes, 11, counting the 0, from 0 to 10. We are also over-simplifying our analogy because in reality, the volume control is a variable slider and can be set anywhere in between whole numbers.) It's not hard imagining that this happened as the result of random movements.

Let's revise and revisit this story.

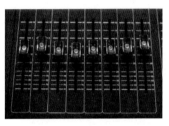

Your sound board has 8 controls (each of which could be set at 11 different settings). Before you leave the studio for the day, you move all of the controls to 0. You have a huge project the next morning, requiring each of the 8 controls to be set at an exact value. You arrive the next day and find all the controls are exactly where they need to be! You ask one of your assistants what happened. They say, "Sorry, my 4-year old son was messing around with the board and he must have done that." Would you believe your assistant this time? You shouldn't! Why not? What changed?

Well, it's no longer a *plausible* story. What are the chances that every control would be set perfectly? We can calculate that very easily. You have 8 controls, each of which could be set at any of 11 different values. Mathematically expressed, that's 11^8 which equals 214,358,881. That means there is only one chance in 214,358,881 that it would happen by random fidgeting. Is that impossible? No, but I would never bet on it! It is a much more likely scenario that someone else knew where the controls needed to be set and intentionally did the work ahead of time. The more factors there are, and the more possible settings there are for each of the factors, the more incredibly unlikely it is that random events can account for the correct outcome.

Leaving our analogies and returning to the real world, we consider the fact that at least 30 finely tuned factors are necessary for the existence of our universe, including the following:

- Electromagnetic force constant
- Electron to proton mass ratio
- The color of our Sun
- Distance of the Earth from the sun
- Size of our moon
- Distance of our moon from the Earth
- Gravitational Constant
- Cosmological Constant

But it's much worse than you think! Our last audio mixer analogy involved 8 controls each of which could be set at any 1 of 11 settings. What we find with these parameters in physics is not just that there are about 4 times more parameters (i.e., sliders), but that some of them have an astronomical number of potential settings, not just 11.

Trying to keep this somewhat simple, imagine adding just 2 more sliders (10 total) and each slider now has double the possible settings (22). The probability moves from one chance in 216 million (as in the previous example) to less than one chance in 26 trillion! Making small changes to our initial conditions yields a HUGE decrease in probability.

Let's go one step further. Instead of increasing the possible settings from 11 to 22, let's consider the possible setting range of a real-life factor; the gravitational constant. The gravitational constant obviously has to do with the force of gravity. It has been estimated that if you had a ruler that spanned across the entire universe (try

finding one at an office supply store!), each inch on the
ruler would represent a possible value for the gravitational
constant. (That equals a bit more than 11 or 22 settings!)
What if the universe popped into existence but the
gravitational constant didn't land where it did? We don't
have to ask what would happen if it was somewhere else
on the ruler halfway across the universe. All we have to
do is consider it being one inch from where it is now.
Animals would be instantly crushed, and insects
would need very thick legs just to support themselves!

So, do we really believe we just got that lucky?

I want to look at one final factor, the cosmological constant, which
is related to the energy density of space. As an important caveat,
the cosmological constant is something directly tied into the Big
Bang model. I do not believe the Big Bang is a scientifically-sound
model for the origin of the universe. I am simply including this
finely tuned factor in my example to show that even if the Big Bang
did happen, this factor is so immensely finely tuned that it could not
have happened by undirected processes.

We will look at what the chances are that undirected forces of nature
set both the previous gravitational constant and this additional
cosmological constant to the very precise values necessary for our
universe. Scientists have done the math for us. It turns out, just
for these two factors, the chances are 1 chance in 10 million trillion
trillion trillion trillion trillion trillion! In case you're at all curious
. . . that's a BIG number! That screams, "This could NOT possibly
happen by chance!"

And that's just for two factors! We could look at many more.

How can anyone possibly deny this evidence? Well, they get pretty creative. In a nutshell, it goes like this. "You creationists are right about the fine-tuning argument. Well, that is, if this was the only universe in existence. However, there are infinite universes out there, so there's bound to be at least one having all the right factors, and we just happen to be living in that one!" Really? Yes, really! That is the main argument against the fine-tuning evidence.

First of all, that response is not even scientific. There's no evidence for an infinite number of universes. We can't even see the boundaries of our own universe, let alone see beyond it to conclude there are others elsewhere. Even if we thought we saw something, how would we know it was a separate universe and not just another portion of our own? We couldn't know that.

I am committed to not writing an entire book on the origin of the universe right now, so I have to wind down.

Conclusion

Both the Laws of Thermodynamics and the anthropic principle's fine-tuning argument strongly support the Christian worldview, but present seemingly insurmountable challenges for the atheistic worldview. Many other lines of evidence could be explored and found to have the same conclusion. Please check out our many video resources for additional information regarding the origin of the universe.

Scientific Example #2: The Variety of Life Forms

Let's begin again with looking at what each worldview purports.

Atheistic Worldview

All the various life forms we see today descended from a common ancestor which existed in the form of a single-cell perhaps 3.8 billion years ago. Each successive life form arose from slight changes to the previous form through mutations and natural selection (i.e., Darwinian evolution).

Christian Worldview

God supernaturally created original kinds of creatures, fully-formed and fully-functional. While they can generate quite a wonderful variety, they always reproduce "after their kind" (Genesis 1:1112, 21, 24-25).

What does the evidence indicate?

So, what do we actually see today? We observe dogs reproducing dogs, cats reproducing cats, alligators reproducing alligators, rabbits reproducing rabbits (and lots of them), etc.! Occasionally, we see interesting hybrids. One example is when a lion and tiger breed resulting in a "liger." This works because the tiger and lion are both of the same genus (*Panthera*). However, you cannot breed a tiger and longhorn sheep, because the sheep is part of a different genus (*ovis*).

We are very aware of genetic information's ability to produce a variety of features, but there are always limits. We can have dogs with short fur, medium length fur or long fur, or even with no fur! However, they are always . . . dogs! In  fact, we can go even further with this. Today, dogs, dingoes, coyotes and wolves can all breed together! Why? Because they are the same "kind" of animal. In this case, they are all classified on the genus level as *canis*.

You can breed a wolf and a dog, and you get . . . a wolf-dog! No surprise. In fact, most scientists (creationist and evolutionist alike) believe that all current 400 or so domestic breeds of dogs originated from something more like a European gray wolf all within approximately the past 200 years! Genetic studies confirm this and it's certainly in accordance with what we would expect from animals reproducing after their own kind.

However, you do not get a German Shepherd or Doberman from a wolf by adding *new* genetic information; you produce these dogs through selective breeding which actually "selects out" certain features. It is a process of *elimination*. Genetic information is *lost* in the process, not gained. A wolf has a greater variety of genetic information than a typical domesticated dog. This is one reason that purebred dogs are generally not as healthy as a "mut" because they are less able to adapt to changes in their environment, and they suffer from mutational defects because of inbreeding. We may like the looks of these purebreds, but we're not really doing them any favors in the long run. (I am not an anti-dog breeding advocate. I am just casually making a simple point.)

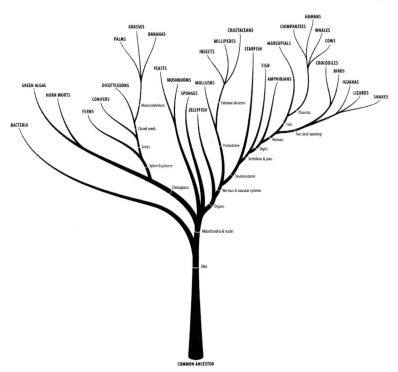

Darwin's famous "tree of life" has fallen greatly out of favor. It depicted a nice, clean, smooth transition from the initial single cell organism, eventually branching out to all other life forms. A picture might be worth a thousand words, but in this case, it's not even worth one truth. Genetics simply does not support this antiquated concept! The new drawing resembles a "bush" much more than a tree with many connections going horizontally, from one branch to another.

Studies in genetics are much more consistent with God creating specific "kinds" of animals fully capable of expressing various features enabling them to fill different niches around the globe. While we see great variety, there are always stark genetic limits. This is certainly not at all what we would expect from an evolutionary viewpoint. We should view a smooth continuum, with it being somewhat difficult to distinguish one form from the next in line.

When evolutionists see a particular gene in a certain species, they attribute its origin to having been inherited from an earlier evolved life form (i.e., lower on the evolutionary tree). There are better explanations for this, such as common design and common necessity. However, the bigger problem is we often find genes in higher life forms that cannot be traced back to any other supposed earlier life form! These are called orphan genes. With the concept of evolution, each gene we discover should simply be a copy or modification of a previously existing gene. When you find many examples in which there are no similar previously existing genes, your theory is in a whole lot of hurt!

For these reasons and a whole host of others, the variety of life on this planet clearly is in line with the biblical narrative but is antithetical to an evolutionary scenario.

Scientific Example #3: The Origin of Information

One more time, let's begin by looking at what each worldview purports.

Atheistic Worldview

All the information we find in various life forms all over the planet came from undirected interactions of particles over billions of years, starting about 3.8 billion years ago (when life arose from non-living chemicals).

Christian Worldview

God supernaturally spoke everything into being, including all the complex information we see in every living thing. "In the beginning was the Word (Greek: *logos*), and the Word was with God, and the Word was God" (John 1:1). I'll share more about this at the end of this section.

What does the evidence indicate?

Consider a newspaper. It's made by using paper and ink. It can hold a lot of information.

Next, think about a book, also made using paper and ink. It can hold even more information than a newspaper.

Now consider a compact disc (CD), made using a combination of plastic and metal. A single CD can hold 100,000 pages of text!

Next consider a computer flash drive, made by using mostly metals and plastic. A 4G (gig) flash drive can hold 6 entire CDs! That's 600,000 pages of text!

Lastly, consider a portable hard drive. A 2T (terabyte) hard drive can hold 500 4G flash drives! That's simply amazing!

In each of these cases, the physical materials do a great job of *storing* information, but in none of these cases did the materials *create* the information. The paper and ink didn't write the newspaper columns or the chapters in the book. A human reporter or author did. The plastic and metal didn't write Microsoft Office software. Numerous software engineers did. They just used those materials to store the immense amount of information. This all makes perfect sense. You can easily see hallmarks of intelligence. It's what allows you to differentiate between random sequences of letters and specified orders of letters conveying meaningful concepts (i.e., words and sentences).

Let's turn our focus now to another physical structure that also contains information — DNA. Each cell in your body (except red blood cells) contains stands of DNA in its nucleus. While being almost unimaginably thin (to fit within such a small, microscopic space), if extracted from a single cell it would be about 6 feet long! Each cell contains virtually the entire complement of information needed to develop your entire body! For example, the DNA in a skin cell on the tip of your finger contains all the information necessary to make your heart, your spine, your brain, etc.! Fortunately, it also knows where it is and what is expected of it — to just make a skin cell here, not to be an over-achiever and start making another liver!

The amount of information in the DNA of each of our cells is equivalent to approximately 3 billion letters! That would be equal to the amount of information found in over 5,000 300-page books! If we look at the storage capacity of DNA, meaning how much data can be stored in a given space, the details are fascinating.

For comparison sake, remember that a single CD can hold 100,000 pages of text. A 4-Gig flash drive can hold 600,000 pages of text. A 2-Terabyte portable hard drive can hold 500 of those flash drives, or 300,000,000 pages of text! While all very impressive, it all pales in comparison to DNA. What if you had just a 2mm pinhead amount of DNA? How much data could be contained within that small space? That's a very, very small volume. Based on my "back of the napkin" calculations, the volume of a typical 2-Terabyte portable hard drive is equivalent to about 13,303 pinheads. So, we're asking how much data can be stored in an amount of DNA that is less than 1/13000th the size of a 2-Terabyte hard drive. It turns out you could store 2 million of these hard drives in a pinhead amount of DNA. Now that's truly impressive!

Every time we observe high volumes of information (e.g., books, hard drives, etc.) we can always trace the information back to an intelligent source. Given that fact, when we see immensely more information within the DNA of living creatures, why would we conclude the volume of intelligent information just assembled by undirected interactions of particles over long periods of time? Call me crazy, and I'm sure many have, but I see that as strong evidence of intelligent design. You have to ask the skeptic, "If the incredible complexity of DNA, which gets more and more complex the more we study it, is not evidence for design, what would be? Seriously. Please give me an example. If you can't tell me what it is you are expecting to see, how will you ever know if you've found it? If you don't have clearly defined criteria of what counts and what doesn't as evidence for intelligent design, we can't even have an honest conversation.

Conclusion

We've just reviewed three scientific phenomena to ask which of the two worldviews intrinsically does a better job accounting for what we observe in each case. We could review countless other examples, but these should suffice in giving you the gist of this line of reasoning. While the atheistic worldview consistently struggled in its efforts, the Christian worldview consistently offered a very natural explanation.

11

Your Assignment

We've covered a lot of ground since the opening pages of this book. Along the way we truly discovered that "faith is not a four-letter word." In fact, it's not a bad word for Christians or non-Christians. Helping people understand this important concept often provides the key to opening a skeptic's heart to truth.

In reality, having faith is a requirement of all belief systems. There aren't any worldviews based purely on demonstrable facts. Even atheists ultimately have faith that God does not exist. I affectionately call them "faithists." It isn't a matter of whether or not you have faith, it's really a matter of the basis of your faith.

While having blind faith is never a good thing, true biblical faith is a confident assurance and is supported by a wealth of evidence. We're all on a spiritual journey. Even though our salvation is an event that happens at a specific point in time, our maturity in the faith is a life-long endeavor.

I certainly have had many memorable moments of growth myself. One of the most impactful was the passing of my parents. I am so incredibly thankful for the role they played in my life and in making me who I am today. Ultimately, God gets all the credit, but He uses people and circumstances along the way and my parents played a critical role.

My parents passed away in 2013 and 2016. I should say they "changed addresses," that sounds so much better and is actually very accurate. I personally placed my trust in Christ as my Savior when I was 5 years old during a Backyard Bible Club led by . . . my mom. Having been raised in a Christian home and having attended solid Bible-believing churches, I have always believed that when Christians die, they go to heaven. Not only did I believe that, I could show you verses in the Bible to back it up. However, it was more on the level of head knowledge than anything else. When my dad passed away, for the first time in my entire life, my faith regarding heaven changed from academically believing it, to truly *knowing* it. In fact, I felt I knew my Dad was in Heaven with as much certainty as anything else! It was so incredibly real; I can't really even explain it. My dad is not here anymore, but I'll get to see him again. I just have to wait a while, that's all.

That confidence carried over to my mom's passing. About 2 days after her funeral, I had a speaking engagement on the Jersey shores. When I began my talk, I mentioned my mom's passing, including that the funeral was just 2 days ago. I could hear an audible "gasp" from the audience, presumably conveying they felt this must be a very difficult time for me. I told them about someone asking me if I thought my mom was in Heaven now. My response was, "No, I don't think so. I *KNOW* she is!" I then went on to explain how we as Christians can be certain regarding God's promises. It's pretty amazing. I can't imagine living life without that certainty, but I know most people on the planet lack this peace that passes all our human understanding (Philippians 4:6-7).

I've Been Holding Out on You!

There's something I've been putting off telling you. "What's that?" you ask nervously. What we've just been through in this book is what is known as "presuppositional apologetics." "Pre-what?"

I didn't tell you right away because I was afraid some of you would run off to go watch paint dry, or anything else that sounds a lot more interesting.

Let me explain. There are two major types of apologetics (i.e., "defending the faith"). One approach is called, "evidential," the other is "presuppositional."

Evidential apologetics is pretty much just what it sounds like it would be. It is primarily using evidence to defend the faith. The gist of it is that you can trust the Christian worldview because there's so much evidence. In other words, we believe Christianity is true because of the evidence. This approach (which I used for years) is very well-intended, but I believe it leads to faulty thinking. In essence, it is saying the evidence has ultimate authority, so we turn to it to determine whether or not our worldview is correct. As we've seen, evidence is subject to interpretation and subject to being overruled by future evidence, so our opinion as to the validity of our faith would always tentative and subservient to the evidence, or more accurately, the interpretation of the evidence.

Furthermore, evidence always has to be interpreted to give it any kind of meaning. The catch is that we always use our current beliefs (i.e., our "starting point," or "worldview") as a means by which we render our interpretation. You have to start with your staring point. . . or it wouldn't be your starting point!

Understanding this, along with what the Bible claims to be (i.e., the authoritative, inspired, inerrant Word of God), we use it to properly understand the evidence and come to the proper conclusions. Presuppositional apologetics is simply using our "presuppositions" (what we pre-suppose to be true, our "starting point") to conduct apologetics (the defense of the faith). Clear as mud? Actually, it should be fairly clear by now after having read this book. It's a concept, that while initially is a bit difficult to process, makes more and more sense the further you think it through. (Review chapter 8 if you are still struggling with this concept.)

Summary Takeaway

Even though skeptics claim to base everything they believe on facts and feel that Christians just blindly and unreasonably choose to believe in fairytales and wishful thinking, we know that is far from the truth. For many people, when you ask them what they believe, they offer a somewhat sketchy description and sometimes attempt to back it up, but it's usually very lacking. When push comes to shove (not literally), they will admit, "Well, that's just what I believe."

Here's a very important question at this point. What seems to make more sense: that God would judge you based on whatever standards you come up with, or that He would judge you based on His standards? I have yet to hear a person tell me they believe God would use whatever standards each person developed on their own. Given this fact, it is very important that people know what God's standards truly are, and that's where you can help!

Call to Action

Picture being part of a meeting where a very important project was being discussed. Many great ideas are shared by numerous attendees, and there's a fair amount of energy and agreement amongst the whole group. Everyone leaves feeling very good about the meeting as they head  back to their desks to continue whatever work they had been doing prior to the meeting. A week later, you find yourself back in another meeting regarding the same project. What has been accomplished since last week? Maybe nothing! Why? Because there was no "call to action." No "next steps" were discussed. No one was assigned any specific tasks, so no one did anything, even though they all agreed what had been discussed was important.

It can be the same way with this book! I am hoping and assuming you learned some valuable lessons during the time spent here. However, if you don't put anything you learned into practice, the time you spent reading could be virtually useless.

This book was not written to help you win arguments! Its main purpose is to help you better understand the Christian faith and clearly see the myth of the "facts vs faith" argument. In turn, you should be better positioned to share and defend your faith when talking to others.

How do non-Christians come to saving faith in Jesus Christ? The first step in someone trusting Jesus Christ is by hearing the Gospel message.

> How then shall they call on Him in whom they have not believed? And how shall they believe in Him of whom they have not heard? And how shall they hear without a preacher? And how shall they preach unless they are sent? As it is written: "How beautiful are the feet of those who preach the gospel of peace, Who bring glad tidings of good things!" But they have not all obeyed the gospel. For Isaiah says, "Lord, who has believed our report?" So then faith comes by hearing, and hearing by the word of God (Romans 10:14-17).

They can't believe until they've heard the truth of the Gospel, but they can't hear unless someone tells them. But how will they hear from you unless you are sent? The idea of being sent has two aspects: (a) being called to go, and (b) following through in obedience to that calling. But what if you haven't been called? Sorry, that one doesn't work. We are all commanded to preach the Gospel and make disciples (Mark 16:15).

> Therefore settle it in your hearts not to meditate beforehand on what you will answer; for I will give you a mouth and wisdom which all your adversaries will not be able to contradict or resist (Luke 21:14-15).

The context of this passage is Jesus talking to the disciples and others in the Temple, warning them of the pending persecution. He doesn't want them to spend any time worrying about what they will say when they are confronted. Jesus promised to give them the proper words; words which no one will be able to refute. We cannot take this out of context to mean that every time we witness to someone, Jesus will magically give us the words to instantly shut down every opposing argument, but it does convey a general principle that the Holy Spirit will guide you as you sincerely strive to remove yourself from center stage and allow God to speak through you (references John 16:13, Romans 8:26-27, 1 Corinthians 2:13).

So, what's your action plan? I can tell you in general what it should be. You'll have to pray about the specifics.

1. Know **WHAT** You Believe

Rehearse in your mind a relatively succinct explanation of the Christian worldview. You don't want to be part of this conversation:
"So, what is it exactly you believe?" "Well, it's kind of like, um, sort of, um. It's hard to describe. I guess I'd say God created everything and Adam sinned, so Jesus is the only way to heaven so you need Him in your heart."

I'm not saying my personal choice of words are magical, but your response could be a bit more meaningful to the skeptic or the atheist if it was more substantial. Here's an example that might relate better to the non-Christian mindset:

The Bible claims to be the inspired Word of God, and there's actually a lot of fascinating evidence for that claim. In it we learn that God created everything to begin with, including you and me. There's a huge amount of scientific evidence for the concept of supernatural creation as well. We learn that Adam and Eve were given a choice to honor God as their Creator or to decide they thought they knew better. Unfortunately, they thought their plan was better than God's and that decision resulted in them being separated from God. It also brought a curse into God's originally perfect creation and we continue to experience the effects of that today. Not only did Adam and Eve mistakenly think they knew better than God, we do the same thing on a fairly regular basis. Since God is 100% Holy, His standard is 100% perfection. That means we could never work hard enough to be good enough to meet that criteria. We always fall short. The good news is that God loves us so much that He decided He would pay the price for our sins Himself. He did so when He sent His own son, Jesus (who was 100% perfect), to die on a cross to pay for the sins of the whole world. However, for that payment to be applied to our personal debt, we need to pray to God, admitting we are sinners and that we can't possibly be good enough on our own merits. We tell God that we accept His free gift as the payment for our sins. It is on that basis alone that we will gain access to heaven when we die. Anything else won't cut it. Unfortunately, all religions around the world are variations of we supposedly need to do to meet some standard set by some human authority to achieve whatever ultimate reward that particular religion offers. True Christianity, on the other hand, is not so much a "religion" but a relationship! It's not about what we do; it's about what Jesus did! It's about having an actual relationship with Him, as opposed to a sterile academic knowledge of Him coupled with just "trying to do our best."

That should be a bit more effective than, "Um, well, kind of like…" It can also lead to some very spiritually important conversations.

2. Know <u>WHY</u> You Believe It

In the previous section, my brief description of what Christianity is all about included claims of evidence for supernatural origin of life and the  universe, as well as evidence for the inspiration of Scripture. You don't need to be an expert in either of these areas, but you do need to be ready to offer an example or two of evidence. Hopefully, you have that takeaway from reading this book.

It is not the focus of this book to elucidate all the evidence, but here's a brief description of one line of evidence from each of two major areas: supernatural creation and inspiration of the Bible.

Creation

It's extremely challenging to pick out just one example from creation, but for our purposes we'll chose the origin of life. Discussing that event should be fairly impactful to those thinking through whether or not life could have arisen on its own through purely undirected processes in nature.

Without fleshing-out all of the detailed scientific hurdles that would have to be overcome to turn non-living chemicals into a living, self-sustaining, reproducing cell, we will simply look at what the probability is for such an event. We don't want to get too hung up on an exact number, since there have been multiple attempts at calculating such a probability, all of which approach it slightly differently. The overall conclusion is that there's no feasible way it could have happened on this planet or anywhere in the universe. The particular figure I will share came from Sir Frederick Hoyle, a British astronomer who was an atheist for most of his life. He calculated that the chances life could have formed purely by natural processes is 1 chance in $10^{40,000}$! Looks like a big number, but exactly how big is that? That is 1 chance in a 1 followed by 40,000 zeros! It's so big it's almost impossible to relate to. Here's an analogy that may help. Most people have played with a Rubik's Cube at some point in their life. There are actually 10 million trillion different combinations to this unique puzzle and only one is correct. That means if you were blindfolded, someone handed you a cube, and you started spinning it randomly, you would have 1 chance in 10 million trillion of getting it right! No sane person would honestly believe they could solve it that way.

Now let's compare solving that cube on the first try to the chance of life forming via natural processes calculated by Sir Fred Hoyle (1 in $10^{40,000}$). It would be like solving the cube blindfolded 2,105 times in a row and getting it right every single time. That's never going to happen! Not even close! The best science we have today indicates that as far as we can tell, life cannot form without outside, intelligent intervention. Oh, some people hope someone will find an answer some day. However, science deals with what we *do* know, not on what we *hope* to find some day. To place hope in a future discovery is an act of faith and at this point, it's an astronomically long stretch and more of a blind faith. The research conducted over the past 70 years has not brought us closer to discovering evidence to substantiate an evolutionary origin of life; it has only revealed additional layers of complexity and more unimaginable barriers to overcome. Here's an interesting admission from Hubert P. Yockey, Evolutionist, PhD physicist & information theorist:

> "The belief that life on earth arose spontaneously from non-living matter, is simply a matter of faith…"[42]

Inspiration of the Bible

When approaching the question regarding the inspiration of the Bible, you can ask the atheist or skeptic a very basic question. "If God actually wrote a book, how would we know? What would we expect to see within its pages?" If someone gave me an article about computers and told me it was written by Bill Gates, I would expect it to be very accurate in virtually everything it covered. If I found glaring errors, especially regarding simple concepts, I would instantly question the alleged authorship. So it is with a book alleged to be "written by" God. (I say "written by" but really mean the actual human writers were directly inspired by God in that everything they wrote was what God intended and is completely accurate and trustworthy.)

So, what do we see when we survey the Bible? We see it is (1) internally consistent (i.e., no contradictions, although many have been alleged), (2) historically accurate, (3) scientifically accurate and (4) prophetically accurate.

Just looking at one of these areas, the Bible is 27% prophetic in its content. That means 27% of the Bible makes predictions about the future. That's over 8,000  passages, making over 1,800 predictions, covering over 700 topics! Some of those prophesies were given to be fulfilled in our future. Every other prophecy has come true in every minute detail! You won't find anything even close to that in any other religious writings out there! If a bunch of ignorant goat-herders and others made up the Bible, how is this 100% accurate fulfilled prophesy possible? The only rational answer is that they didn't make it up. They were inspired by God in everything they wrote. Space doesn't allow me to go into numerous examples, but we produced an entire 5-part video series entitled, *Inspiration of the Bible*, in which I cover each one of the four areas mentioned above.

3. Pray for Opportunities to Witness

Generally speaking, I would not recommend making deals with God. (Mainly, because God is not in a position where He needs to make deals with us. Secondarily, because there's too much of a chance that we will not live up to our end of the bargain!)

In this case, the "deal" is somewhat tongue-in-cheek and is not something that is clearly contrary to any biblical teaching. It's a 2-for-1 deal that I made with God years ago and this is how it goes.

I prayed and told God if anytime I met someone He would (a) clearly let me know if this is a person He wants me to witness to right then, and (b) give me a somewhat natural opening into a conversation, I would jump on it, trusting Him for the right words to say.

Warning! Don't pray this unless you mean it because God will never drop the ball! Every time I've prayed that prayer, He has followed through on His end. In my case, it's usually me praying that prayer as I am preparing to fly somewhere to speak. It almost always involves speaking with someone on the plane. Whenever someone sits next to me, my spirit always clearly knows whether or not "this is the person." Once I sense the affirmation from the Holy Spirit, I am always praying, "Ok God, how do we do this thing?" Sure enough, something always happens that leads to a comfortable conversation and I naturally am able to share the Gospel with them. It has never been awkward, even though it wasn't always easy to begin with. You simply have to be willing and available. The Holy Spirit does all the heavy lifting! And it gets easier and easier the more you do it. And the more you do it, the more you *want* to do it! There's nothing quite like sharing the Gospel with someone, even when they aren't extremely receptive. You're still sharing the truth and it's not up to you to force the outcome. You're just the messenger. It's not "your philosophy" you're sharing, it's the Word of God!   Big difference!

4. Be on the Lookout!

Lastly, after praying for God to grant you witnessing opportunities, be on the lookout for them. They can come at any time, even those times when you least expect it. I've spontaneously witnessed to delivery people, carpet installers, handymen, guys at the gym, you name it. I've also been able to do that without becoming one of those people that no one wants to make eye contact with.

You'll be surprised how often you could easily get into a spiritually related conversation, often just by asking follow-up questions to what someone said. Someone says, "Yeah, I just got back from my uncle's funeral. He was only 61." You could say, "Sorry to hear about that. That's not very old. You ever wonder about what happens to us when we die? Do you think it's even possible to know?" See where the conversation goes. Another time someone might comment on how crazy the world is getting. You could ask, "Where do you think it's all headed? Ever wonder why we're even here?" Again, their response will probably be very interesting and will give you ample opportunity for deeper, more spiritually related conversation.

Need More Help?

I hope this book has helped you in many ways, but you probably still have more questions. In fact, some of those questions possibly came as a result of reading this book. If there's any way we can be of further assistance, we would love to hear from you. We offer free seminars, sermons, conference, etc., so contact us for more information or to schedule an engagement in your area.

Jay Seegert
The Starting Point Project
TheStartingPointProject.com
info@TheStartingPointProject.com

APPENDIX A

The Nature of Starting Points

I don't want to go into this too deeply, but the basic premise is very important, and it may clear up questions some of you have.

I state in the main text of this book that there's no way to avoid starting somewhere with your belief system. I can't imagine anyone would argue with that. It seems very straight-forward. However, it's also important to realize that starting points cannot be proven to be true using traditional methods. This is due to the nature of starting points, which are also known as presuppositions. Things that can be experienced through one or more of your five senses can be proven by traditional, empirical methods. If you want to know which has greater mass, a cubic inch of lead or a cubic inch of cotton, you can go into a laboratory and put each of them on a scale and see for yourself. (I won't keep you guessing. It's lead. Yes, lead is denser than cotton. Now you're wondering how dense I am!)

When you perform experiments such as this, you are employing outside sources to determine the answer to your question. This presupposes these sources carry with them a certain level of reliable authority. For example, the scale is believed to be manufactured properly and is in good working order. You would also be using a ruler to determine if the objects being weighed were truly each one cubic inch in volume. This presupposes the ruler is accurate. There are other factors as well, some of which you don't normally even think about. At some point, some authoritative body set the standard for how long an inch would be. You are also assuming your eyes are accurately perceiving the markings on the ruler and scale, that your brain is accurately understanding this information and that your hand is then accurately recording the results on paper or typing it correctly into the computer, etc. But it gets even deeper. You are assuming not only the existence of the laws of science, but also assuming their consistency and regularity. You assume that the gravitational constant will be the same tomorrow as it is today. You also assume that this value in physics is the same where you are as it is across town, across the country and across the globe. But how do you test the laws of logic and science without using the laws of logic and science? Interesting question!

Confession Time

I have a confession to make. Actually, it's more along the lines of being very transparent. As we mature in our faith, we should be continually refining the way we share our faith with others. I am currently 53 years into my journey as a  Christian, having placed my trust in Christ when I was just five years old. I spent the past 35 years studying apologetics and working on evangelism. I've learned a lot along the way and have certainly had to make numerous corrections and refinements. That leads me to being transparent related to our current topic – sharing why we believe what we believe.

My views regarding proving the existence of God have "evolved."

In my early apologetics life, I was very quick to say that I had proof of God's existence. I would then share scientific evidence that I felt constituted "proof." Later, I realized these scientific evidences had three major shortcomings.

1. Scientific conclusions have to be considered tentative, since nothing in science is ever truly final. We keep learning more and more and it's certainly at least possible we might discover something that would negate something we earlier deemed to be true. That's just the nature of science. (See chapter 4 for more information, if you haven't reviewed it yet.)

2. Science involves interpreting data. However, we always use what we already believe (our starting points or presuppositions) to drive the interpretation. It's not science that determines our presuppositions, it's our presuppositions that drives our scientific conclusions.

3. Science can only comment on things of a physical nature. The Christian God, by definition, is a spirit, having no physical characteristics or properties. Therefore, science cannot comment directly on God's existence (i.e., through the scientific method involving testing, observation and experimentation, etc.).

So, I went from claiming the existence of God could be proven, to stating that although we cannot technically prove it, the evidence is so overwhelming that the existence of God is by far the most rational conclusion.

But I wasn't done yet. I was thinking too much "inside the box." In reality, the existence of God can be proven, but not by using traditional, empirical methods, which I had been limiting myself to. I will elaborate on this a bit further.

A Different Breed

Starting points are of a different nature than physical entities with which we can perform laboratory experiments. They deal with things we cannot directly sense through sight, touch, hearing, taste, or smell. When you think about the nature of God, you quickly realize He cannot be experienced directly through these senses. You certainly can detect all sorts of things about what He has created, but God Himself is a spirit and there is nothing physical about His nature. Therefore, we should not expect to use these physical senses in an attempt to prove His existence. Does this mean we cannot prove God's existence? Actually, we *can* prove the existence of God, but it involves an internal critique, as opposed to experimentation. In short, the existence of God is proven by the impossibility of the contrary. By what? I'll explain.

It is a well-known logical principal that if two and only two options (A and B) are possible for a given situation and they are mutually exclusive, if "A" turns out to be false, "B" is automatically true by default and by definition. It's actually pretty straightforward.

Let's take a look at a simple example. Don't over think this. Consider a lamp that is either on or off. (No dimmer settings or anything fancy.) If someone was investigating to see if the lamp was on yesterday, and they found out there was no electrical power supplied to the house for the past 4 days due to a power outage in the area (and the owners didn't have a generator), they could conclude the lamp could not have been on. Since there are only two possibilities (on or off), if we have shown the impossibility of one option (i.e., the lamp could not have been on due to the lack of power) we have, therefore, proven it was off. Since it was impossible for the lamp to be on, it must have been off. This is using the concept of "the impossibility of the contrary."

In Chapter 9, I develop this a bit further and conclude that if God does not exist, we have no legitimate justification for the existence of the laws of logic or the laws of science. However, it is impossible to offer a defense for one's beliefs without appealing to logic. The fact that we actually can appeal to logic and the laws of science constitutes proof for God's existence because of "the impossibility of the contrary." That is to say, if God didn't exist, you couldn't legitimately account for the laws of logic or laws of science. Again, Chapter 9 will help you understand this better.

My Journey

So, I went from saying you can prove God's existence, so saying you can't, to saying you can! Did the truth change during my journey? No, just my understanding of the truth. I share this in hopes that it will be an encouragement to you. Everyone goes through similar situations regarding various issues, and some of them are very significant issues. Occasionally, it can even be messy. In my case (as of the writing of this book) the DVD I produced with the same title as this book, contains phraseology reflecting my prior understanding. I am not sure when I will have time to update that video, so for now, I will have to live with the incongruity in presentations (book vs DVD). Fortunately, it is not something monumental, but more of a refinement.

The point is to be in continual prayer and reading of Scripture. It also helps to pursue advice from those who have gone before you and may have insights that will greatly benefit you. I personally received counsel regarding these issues from Dr. Jason Lisle (astrophysicist, Biblical Science Institute), who offered his endorsement on the back cover. He is one of the leading presuppositional apologists, so it was an honor to have his assistance and approval.

> Listen to counsel and receive instruction, That you may be wise in your latter days (Proverbs 19:20).

> Where there is no counsel, the people fall; But in the multitude of counselors there is safety (Proverbs 11:14).

> Without counsel, plans go awry, But in the multitude of counselors they are established (Proverbs 15:22).

One Additional Refinement

There's one more area in which I needed tweak my teaching. It has to do with the inspiration of the Bible. Until recently, here's what I used to say:

> God doesn't need us defending His Word. It's been said, the reason you don't need to defend God's Word is the same reason you don't need to defend a lion. You just let it loose . . . it defends itself. So, we don't go about defending God's Word, we just need to share it with others. It will defend itself. What we do offer along the way is a powerful defense of why *we* have come to the conclusion the Bible is actually the Inspired Word of God. In other words, why *we* believe it's true. That's what apologetics is really all about.

Here's the "problem." When I share reasons why I have chosen to believe the Bible is the Word of God, I am, in reality, defending God's Word! I think I was trying a bit too hard in making a distinction that didn't really exist. The distinction between defending the Bible and defending reasons why I believe the Bible. They are really one and the same. For some reason, I didn't realize this. I think I was too busy trying to know something about everything so that I can respond to just about anyone at any time. My intentions were good, but if I want to grow in my faith and in my effectiveness in witnessing and mentoring others, I need to refine this area as well.

> But sanctify the Lord God in your hearts, and always be ready to give a defense to everyone who asks you a reason for the hope that is in you, with meekness and fear (1 Peter 3:15).

Giving an answer regarding the reason I have hope is truly sharing proof that God exists and defending the Bible as being the inspired Word of God.

Notes

Chapter 1, Introduction – No Notes

Chapter 2, The "Facts vs Faith" Dilemma

1. Stanley Fish, "*Citing Chapter and Verse: Which Scripture Is the Right One?*" The New York Times, *Opinionator*, March 26, 2012, https://opinionator.blogs.nytimes.com/2012/03/26/citing-chapter-and-verse-which-scripture-is-the-right-one/

Chapter 3, Science: What It Is and What It Ain't

2. Sam Harris, Letter to a Christian Nation, (New York: Knopf, 2006).

3. Friedrich Nietzsche, The Joyful Science, (Germany, 1882).

4. Richard Dawkins, Untitled Lecture, Edinburgh Science Festival (1992).

5. Mark Twain, Citation Unknown.

6. Matthew Henry (1662-1714), Commentary on Hebrews, as discussed on Blue Letter Bible Website, https://www.blueletterbible.org/Comm/mhc/Hbr/Hbr_011.cfm

Chapter 4, Science: What It Is and What It Ain't

7. Grigg, Russell, "Enigma Man: A Stone Age Mystery", July 5, 2014; Article on Creation Ministries International Website, https://creation.com/enigma-man Discussion of the Australian TV documentary, *Enigma Man: A Stone Age Mystery*, ABCTV-1 Broadcast on June 24, 2014.

8. Lewontin, R., "Billions and Billions of Demons", The New York Review, January 9, 1997, p. 31.

9. Rennie, John, "15 Answers to Creationist Nonsense," Scientific American, Jul 2002.

10. Darwin, Charles, Origin of Species (New York: D. Appleton and Company, 1859), p. 2.

11. Scott, Eugenie, Quote from AZ Quotes Website. Accessed June 2021. https://www.azquotes.com/quote/694742t

12. Chen, Jun-Yuan Chen, Quote from the 1999 International Symposium on the Origins of Animal Body Plans and Their Fossil Records, Kunming, China, Evolution News Website, April 16, 2014, par. 3. https://evolutionnews.org/2014/04/in_china_we_can/t

13. Richards, Professor Evelleen, Science Historian, University of NSW, Australia, Lateline, 9 October 1998, Australian Broadcasting Corporation. Article on the Creation Ministries International Website. https://creation.com/science-a-reality-check

14. Epstein, Zach, "180,000-year-old human fossil discovery changes what we thought we knew about mankind's history", BGR Website, January 26, 2018. https://bgr.com/2018/01/26/oldest-human-fossil-outside-africa-discovery-50000-years-earlier/

15. Woodward, Aylin, "A handful of recent discoveries have shattered anthropologists' picture of where humans came from, and when", Business Insider Website, January 26, 2018. https://www.businessinsider.com/discoveries-change-picture-of-human-history-evolution-2020-01

16. The Sun, a News UK Company, "JAW DROPPING Fossil found that could change everything we know about the first humans", January 26, 2018. https://www.thesun.co.uk/tech/5429367/oldest-human-fossil-found-outside-africa/

17. Bennett, Alan, Evolution Revolution: Evolution is True. Darwin is Wrong. This Changes Everything (Los Angeles, California: Lexem Publishing, May 2014).

18. "THE TRUTH ABOUT DINOSAURS", Time Magazine, Cover Story, April 26, 1993.

19. Briggs, Helen, Science Correspondent, "New light shed on Charles Darwin's 'abominable mystery'", BBC News, Jan 23, 2021. https://www.bbc.com/news/science-environment-55769269

20. Buggs, Richard, Professor of Evolutionary Genomics at the Queen Mary University of London, Quote from Letter written by Charles Darwin to Dr. Joseph Hooker in 1879. https://www.bbc.com/news/science-environment-55769269

Chapter 5, When Science Gets It Wrong!

21. Grigg, Russell, "Ignaz Semmelweis: Medical pioneer persecuted for telling the truth", Creation Ministries International Website, Last Updated April 2016. https://creation.com/semmelweis

22. World Health Organization (COVID-19 Deaths Worldwide as of June 29, 2021) https://covid19.who.int/

23. Seegert, Jay, *Evolution: Probable or Problematic?* DVD, The Starting Point Project Website. http://thestartingpointproject.mybigcommerce.com/evolution-probable-or-problematic/

24. Mattick, Professor John, University of Queensland, Brisbane, Australia, "Genius of Junk (DNA)", ABC TV science program Catalyst, Broadcast July 10, 2003. https://www.abc.net.au/catalyst/genius-of-junk-dna/11007394

Chapter 6, Ultimate Authority – No Notes

Chapter 7, Suggested Approach – No Notes

Chapter 8, Evidence Is Not Proof

25. Sills, Jennifer, Editor, "Climate Change and the Integrity of Science", Science Magazine, Vol 328, May 7, 2010, Last accessed February 1, 2021. http://www.sciencemag.org/content/328/5979/689.full.pdf

26. Kanazawa, Satoshi, The Scientific Fundamentalist, "Common Misconceptions About Science I: 'Scientific Proof' — Why there is no such thing as a scientific proof", Psychology Today, November 16, 2008. https://www.psychologytoday.com/us/blog/the-scientific-fundamentalist/200811/common-misconceptions-about-science-i-scientific-proof

27. University of California-Berkeley, "Misconceptions about science", Understanding Science, par. 22, Last accessed February 1, 2021. http://undsci.berkeley.edu/teaching/misconceptions.php#b10

28. Dawkins, Richard, The Blind Watchmaker (New York: W.W. Norton & Company, 1986), p. 1.

29. Crick, Dr. Francis (Nobel Prize Laureate in Physiology and Medicine), What Mad Pursuit, (New York: Basic Books, 1988), p.138.

30. Crick, Dr. Francis, Life Itself: Its Origin and Nature, (New York, NY: Simon & Schuster, 1981), p. 88.

31. Hawking, S.W. and Ellis, G.F.R., The Large Scale Structure of Space-Time, (Cambridge, England: Cambridge University Press, 1973), p. 134.

Chapter 9, Philosophy through the Prism of Worldviews

32. Harrison, Peter, "The Bible and the Rise of Science," Australasian Science, Vol. 23, Issue 3, April 2002, (Queensland, Australia: Control Publications), pp.14–15.

33. Stark, Rodney, <u>For the Glory of God: How Monotheism Led to Reformations, Science, Witch-hunts and the End of Slavery</u>, (Princeton, New Jersey: Princeton University Press, 2003), p. 376.

34. Craig, William Lane vs. Brown, James Robert, "Does God Exist?" Live debate in Canada, Thursday, February 19, 2009, Uploaded by Brian Auten, Director of Reasonable Faith Belfast and Founder of Apologetics 315, to the Apologetics 315 Website, Last accessed May 2021. <u>http://apologetics315.blogspot.com/2009/02/william-lane-craig-vs-james-robert.html</u>

35. McIntyre, Andrew, "The Truth about Mao" (Book Review of <u>Mao: The Unknown Story</u>, June 22, 2006), <u>National Observer</u>, No. 67, Summer 2006, pp. 49-55.

Chapter 10, Science through the Prism of Worldviews

36. Somin, Ilya, "Remembering the Biggest Mass Murder in the History of the World", <u>Washington Post</u>, August 3, 2016.

37. Krauss, Lawrence, Interview by Ross Anderson, "Has Physics Made Philosophy and Religion Obsolete?", <u>The Atlantic</u>, April 2012.

38. Krauss, Lawrence, Tyson, Neil deGrasse, Moderator of 2013 Isaac Asimov Memorial Debate: "The Existence of Nothing", Location: American Museum of Natural History, March 22, 2013, at Time Code: 1:01:16, Last accessed May 2021. <u>https://www.youtube.com/watch?v=1OLz6uUuMp8&ab_channel=AmericanMuseumofNaturalHistory</u>

39. Krauss, Lawrence, "Why Is There Something Rather Than Nothing?" BBC Interview, November 6, 2014. http://www.bbc.com/earth/story/20141106-why-does-anything-exist-at-all

40. Einstein, Albert, Good Reads Quotable Quotes, Last accessed June 2021. https://www.goodreads.com/quotes/16479-once-you-can-accept-the-universe-as-matter-expanding-into

41. White, E.B., Charlotte's Web (New York: Harper & Brothers, 1952), p. 28. https://cleveracademy.vn/wp-content/uploads/2016/10/Charlotte_s_Web_.pdf

Chapter 11, Your Assignment

42. Yockey, Hubert P., Information Theory and Molecular Biology, (Cambridge, England: Cambridge University Press, 1992), p. 284.